MORE
OBJECT LESSONS
FROM NATURE

JOANNE E. DE JONGE

BAKER BOOK HOUSE
Grand Rapids, Michigan 49516

MORE
OBJECT LESSONS
FROM NATURE

Contents

Introduction

If you page through this book briefly, you'll find that the objects used are very common and accessible. You should have no trouble finding these visual aids from nature. But more importantly, the children will be reminded of the lesson again and again as they come across these common natural objects. A few common household items (both natural and non-natural) are also included as a convenience for you and for use at times when the children are likely to remain indoors for extended periods.

The first thirty-two lessons can be used in any season; the objects are always available. Lessons 33 through 41 are best used in spring and/or summer; Lessons 42 and 43 work best during autumn. The final nine lessons have been designed for special days but use objects that are available any time of the year.

The lessons themselves are flexible. An "old hand" can use them as suggestions for points and rearrange them to fit an individual style. In several cases alternate ideas are given. But they are written in such a way that a so-called beginner lacking self-confidence can repeat them verbatim. "Stage directions" are often given to help the faint of heart.

Page through the book and acquaint yourself with it for a few minutes. It's my hope that you will be able to use it for a year. And in using it, may you and the children find that the natural objects we find in our own backyards speak eloquently of their Creator.

1

Cactus Christians

Scripture: I have hidden your word in my heart that I might not sin against you (Ps. 119:11).

Concept: We should store God's Word in our hearts.

Objects: A healthy cactus in a pot, a Bible

Who knows what this plant is called? *(Show them the cactus and pause for response.)* That's right. It's a cactus!

Almost everybody knows what a cactus is. A cactus is a rather tough plant with sharp spines on it. *(Show them the spines.)* That's what people remember about a cactus. But there's something neat about a cactus that you can't see, and that's what I want to tell you about.

A cactus stores water inside of its body! If I would take this cactus and cut it open—I'm not going to, because I don't want to ruin the plant—but if I did cut it open, we would find lots of water inside of it.

Not all plants are like that. Many plants take a little drink of water and don't bother to store it up. But a cactus is different. It stores water right inside its body.

You see, it has long, long roots that are hidden just under the ground. *(Stretch out your arms horizontally to indicate long, shallow roots.)* Whenever a little bit of water falls on the ground, these roots grab the water. *("Grab" with your fingers.)* The water travels through the roots and into the body of the cactus. *(Indicate the direction.)* And the cactus stores the water there, so that it can drink later. If more water falls, the roots grab that, too, and store it. Those roots will grab any little bit of water that falls, and the cactus will store it.

Water is very precious to this little plant. It seems to know that it can't live without water; it grabs any little bit that falls near it. And it stores that precious water inside its body.

That's why cactuses live so long and are such hardy plants. At times when other plants wither and die because there's not enough rain, a cactus lives on perfectly well, because it has stored water inside of itself.

In a way, God wants each one of us to act like a cactus. Not on the outside—he doesn't want us to be tough and prickly! But he wants us to act like cactuses on the *inside.* He wants us to store something on the inside.

He wants us to store his Word inside of us! The Bible often talks about storing God's Word in our hearts.

Where can we find God's Word? *(Hold up the Bible and pause for response.)* That's right, God's Word is in the Bible. God wants us to know what he says in the Bible, and to store that in our hearts, to remember that. So, what should we do when someone reads the Bible to us? *(Pause for response.)* Yes! We should listen very carefully. And we should try to remember what we hear. When we listen very carefully, we're like those little cactus roots, grabbing water. *(Indicate the roots grabbing water, as you did before.)* Only, *we're* grabbing God's Word with our ears.

And when we try to remember God's Word, we're like this cactus, storing the water in its body. Only, we're storing God's Word in our hearts.

If we do that, if we listen to God's Word and store it in our hearts, we're storing something very precious to us. God's Word tells us how to live, just like water helps this cactus live. If we store enough of it in our hearts, God's Word will help us live well, even when tough times come.

So, from now on, when you see a cactus like this *(indicate the cactus)*, you can think, "That's just how God wants me to live." God wants you to listen very carefully to the Bible when it's read. *(Indicate cactus roots grabbing water.)* And remember what he says. *(Indicate "storing" something in your heart.)* He wants you to store his Word in your heart.

2

Cares Are Like the Clouds

Scripture: Cast all your anxiety on him because he cares for you (1 Peter 5:7).

Concept: We should give our worries to God.

Object: A picture of clouds (or clouds themselves if the children can see them)

Can you all see what I have in this picture? [*Or* "Can you all see what's floating in the sky outside?"] That's right—*clouds!* They really look heavy and dark [or soft and fluffy]. They look like you could sit on them and dangle your feet over the edge. I'd hate to have one of those break open over my head [if they're dark and heavy]. From where we're sitting, don't those clouds look really solid?

Let me tell you something: Clouds aren't solid at all. No matter what they look like from down here, there's really not much to them. They're made up of air and water, that's all. Birds can fly through them; so can planes. When you fly through a cloud, it looks foggy, and that's all. Clouds simply aren't solid; there's not much to them.

We can learn a lot from these clouds in the sky, because we have clouds in our lives, too. They're very much like the clouds in the sky. By "clouds in our lives" I mean things that we worry about.

Do you ever worry? I think everyone does. Maybe you worry about the first day of school, or if your friends are going to play with you, or whom you're going to sit next to in Sunday school. *(If time permits, you can ask the children to tell a few of their worries.)* Did you know that those worries are just like these clouds? They look big, and if we concentrate on them, we can almost imagine that they're heavy, and that there's a lot to them. But, when we get right up next to them—when the day that we were worrying about dawns—we find out that they're not so bad after all. We really didn't have to worry. Everything seems to take care of itself.

Actually, everything doesn't really just take care of itself. God takes care of those things for us. He told us in the Bible that he would. The Bible tells us to give all our worries to God because he cares for us. And Jesus even told us not to worry about things that we think are going to happen. He will take care of them for us. Jesus doesn't want us to spend our time worrying; instead we can trust him to care for us.

So, the next time you start worrying about something that you think may happen *(mention some of the worries the children listed)*, think about the clouds. They look solid from far away, but there's really not much to them. Then remember that Jesus told us not to worry. Bring your cares to him, and then have a happy day in his love.

3

The Most Important Ingredient

Scripture: If I have the gift of prophecy and can fathom all mysteries and all knowledge, and if I have a faith that can move mountains, but have not love, I am nothing (1 Cor. 13:2).

Concept: Love is the most important ingredient in a Christian's life.

Objects: An empty flower pot, a small bag of soil, a glass of water, and a packet of seeds

I'm going to plant some flowers. I've done this before, and nothing grew. So I'm going to try again, with your help. I'd like you to watch very closely and tell me what I'm doing wrong.

(Show them the flower pot.) I have a good pot. I cleaned it to make sure that there were no bugs that might harm the plant in it. It has holes in the bottom to let out any extra water I might pour on.

(Show them the soil.) This is supposed to be very good soil for growing flowers. I dug it from my gar-

den, and flowers grow well there. So this soil should be fine.

I put the soil into the pot. *(As you speak, do all the things you talk about.)* I won't quite fill the pot. That will give the roots room to grow. Now I press the soil down a bit. Now I give it some water. Now, all I have to do is put it in a sunny spot for a while and make sure I keep watering it. My flowers should grow, right? *(Pause for response.)*

Did I hear someone say that they're not going to grow? My other plants didn't grow either. Why not? *(Pause for response.)*

That's right, I forgot something. I didn't put any seeds in the pot. I can't expect any flowers to grow without planting seeds, can I? I could water this soil every day, and make sure it gets plenty of sunlight, and do everything right, but not a thing will grow, because I forgot the most *important* ingredient—the seeds. Without the seeds, no matter what I do, I'll grow nothing in the pot.

I was kidding about having done this before. I just wanted you to watch very closely, so that you would remember that this pot is nothing without the seeds.

You see, in a way, each one of us is like this pot. God wants us to grow and flower as Christians. And he's given us all the directions in the Bible. He even told us not to forget the most important thing—love. *(Show them the packet of seeds.)*

Love is like these seeds. We can do everything right in our lives. We can listen to the Bible; we can pray to God; we can go through all the motions of being nice to others; but if we don't have love in our hearts, we'll be like this pot. *(Show them the pot you just "planted.")* We'll be empty. The Bible says that without love, we are nothing. Just as you can't expect a plant to grow in this pot without seeds, so you can't expect to grow a life pleasing to God without love. God says that the most important ingredient is love—for Jesus and for others. Without that we are nothing.

But if we put love in our lives, love for Jesus and others deep in our hearts *(plant the seeds in the pot)*, then we can grow as Christians pleasing to God.

Now this pot is complete. I've planted the seeds. And if you have love in your heart you, too, will grow into a complete Christian in God's love. Love is the most important ingredient.

4

Cabbage Christians

Scriptures: Finally, brothers, whatever is true, whatever is noble, whatever is right, whatever is pure, whatever is lovely, whatever is admirable—if anything is excellent or praiseworthy—think about such things (Phil. 4:8).

Concept: God wants us to be good on the inside as well as the outside.

Object: A head of cabbage

I brought a head of cabbage with me because there's something really neat about cabbage that I want to show you. *(Show them the cabbage. Keep it up where they can see it as you talk about it.)*

Here's the whole head, just as I found it in the store. It looks pretty good for cabbage, doesn't it? All these outer leaves look healthy. There are no bruises or little holes in them. They're fine to pull off and cook if I want cabbage. *(Pull off a few outer leaves.)*

When I pull off these outer leaves, we find the same thing inside—more leaves. I can pull these off *(pull off the second layer of leaves)*, and what do we find under them? The same thing—more leaves. If I pull these leaves off *(pull off the next layer of leaves)*, what do we find? *(Pause for response.)* That's right, the same thing—more leaves! And if I pull these leaves off we find . . . *(pause for response)* . . . the same thing.

If I kept pulling these layers away, what do you suppose I would find underneath them? *(Pause for response.)* That's right, always the same thing! With this cabbage what you see is what you get. There are leaves on the inside just like on the outside. I could just keep pulling away the same kind of leaves until I pulled the whole cabbage apart.

That's what I think is so neat about a cabbage. The inside is exactly like the outside. There are no surprises. You know what's inside by looking at the outside. It's the same through and through.

That's the way God wants us to be—the same through and through.

We all know that God wants us to live good lives. He wants us to love each other; to be kind, helpful, generous, good people. That's the part that people see, like the outer leaves of this cabbage.

But God also tells us to be good on the inside, where people can't see. The Bible says that whatever is true and noble and right and pure and lovely, that's what we should think about.

People can't see what we think, can they? Our thoughts are kind of like the inner leaves of this cabbage. No one can see them when the cabbage is whole. They could be bad, and no one would know the difference. But God can see us on the inside as well as the outside. And he wants our thoughts to be lovely and pure. He wants us to be good through and through.

18

He wants us to be the same on the inside as well as the outside, just like this cabbage.

So, when you're being kind, helpful, generous, and good to people, put your whole heart into it. And if you're tempted to think bad thoughts while you're good on the outside, think about the cabbage. It's good through and through, the same on the inside as well as the outside. Try to be a cabbage Christian.

5

To You, from God

Scripture: All Scripture is God-breathed and is useful for teaching, rebuking, correcting and training in righteousness, so that the man of God may be thoroughly equipped for every good work (2 Tim. 3:16, 17).

Concept: The Bible is God's personal Word to us.

Objects: A letter in an envelope, a Bible

Look what I got in the mail this week! *(Show them the letter. Take it out of the envelope and unfold it as you speak.)* I love to get personal mail like this. It keeps me in touch with friends that I don't see often.

This letter is from [name]. In it he/she tells me what he's doing, asks me a few questions, and tells me once again that he is a good friend [or, that he loves me]. I think I've read this letter three times already this week. I always read my personal letters more than once. I really enjoy getting them.

How many of you would like to get a letter like this, addressed to you, in your mailbox this week? *(Raise your hand as you ask the question to encourage a similar response.)* I think we all like to get letters from friends.

How many of you think that you *will* get a letter this week? *(Don't raise your hand this time. Pause slightly to see if anyone raises a hand.)* I doubt that I'll get another one so soon. Letters like this just don't come to us very often. *(Put the letter back into the envelope.)*

Yet, I have a surprise for you. Each one of you has a very important personal letter waiting right here for you. It's meant just for you, and it was written by someone who knows you very well and loves you very much. *(Show them the Bible.)* Here's your personal letter; it's the Bible!

Who does the Bible come from? *(Pause for response.)* That's right; it comes from God. And who is it meant for? *(Pause for response.)* Yes, it's meant for you, and you, and you! *(Point at individual children as you speak. Include their names if you can.)*

God gives you all sorts of news in the Bible, and it's all Good News. He tells you that he made the world and everything in it. He tells you that Jesus came into the world to save you. He tells you that Jesus is coming again. And he tells you over and over again that he loves you.

We hear the Bible read so often, sometimes we forget that it's God's personal letter to us. Maybe it will help if I read a few verses to you, just like a letter. *(Open the Bible to these passages.)*

Dear _____, (Use the name of a child in your audience.) "Never will I leave you; never will I forsake you" (Heb. 13:5). Love, GOD.

Dear _____, "Are not two sparrows sold for a penny? Yet not one of them will fall to the ground apart from the will of your Father. And even the very hairs of your head are all numbered. So don't be afraid; you are worth more than many sparrows" (Matt. 10:29-31). Love, GOD.

Dear _____ and _____ and _____, "A new command I give you: Love one another. As I have loved you, so you must love one another" (John 13:34). Love, JESUS.

You can do that yourself the next time someone reads the Bible to you. Before they start, you can say "Dear _____," and put your own name there. When they finish, you can sign it off with "Love, GOD" or "Love, JESUS." That will help you remember that this Bible is God's personal letter to you.

And when the mail carrier comes to your house this week with letters *(hold up the letter with one hand)*, it won't matter if there's nothing for you. Because you already have the very best personal letter *(hold up the Bible with the other hand)*, sent to you from God.

6

The Thorns of Life

Scripture: . . . though now for a little while you may have had to suffer grief in all kinds of trials. These have come so that your faith . . . may be proved genuine and may result in praise, glory and honor when Jesus Christ is revealed (1 Peter 1:6, 7).

Concept: Troubles can strengthen a Christian's faith.

Object: A rose with the thorns still on the stem

I think a rose is one of the most beautiful flowers found on God's green earth, don't you? *(Hold the rose up while you talk about it.)* The color is gorgeous, the petals can look like velvet, and the flower looks almost perfect to me. And it smells nice. It smells so good that people often try to make perfumes out of it.

But there's one thing about a rose that's not so nice. Can anyone tell me what it is? *(Pause for response.)* That's right; it has thorns. *(Point out the thorns on the stem as you speak.)* You have to be careful if you pick a rose, because those thorns can give you a nasty little poke. That's just the way a rose is; it's beautiful, but it has thorns.

Although we might not like those thorns, they do serve a purpose. They protect the rose. None of us is going to pick roses without thinking twice, because we know that the bush is covered with thorns. And animals don't often chew on wild rose bushes. They know that the bush has thorns that can hurt their mouths, so they stay away from it. The thorns protect the roses.

So we may not like the thorns, but they are there for a purpose. And we all know that if you want a rose, you have to put up with the thorns; that's just the way it is.

This rose with its thorns can remind us of our lives. It's often great, but there are thorns. That sounds strange, doesn't it? Let me explain.

God is good to all of us. He gives us enough food, good families, and good homes to live in. He says that he loves us and that he will always take care of us. That's beautiful, just like this rose is beautiful.

But there are a few thorns. God never promised us that our lives would be free from trouble. Things happen to us and make us sad. That's like the thorns on this stem. They're going to happen; that's a part of life.

Sometimes you become sick; that's not fun but it happens. *(Point to the thorns on the stem as you speak.)* That's like a thorn. Or your best friend may move away from your neighborhood. Another thorn. Or your pet may die. Another thorn.

You get the idea, don't you? I'm not going to list all the sad things that happen to you, but things are going to happen that will be sad. That's just the way life is; it's like a rose with thorns.

Yet God tells us that even those "thorns," the not-so-nice things that happen, can bring you closer to God and make your faith in Jesus as strong as possible.

Every time that something not-so-nice happens, you can pray to God to help you and be near to you. He's promised that he will. When you become ill, you can pray to Jesus to help you become healthy again. And you will be reminded just how much we rely on God to help us.

When a best friend moves away, or when it seems like you have no friends in the world, you can pray to Jesus. He's promised to be near you always. You can learn what a friend Jesus is.

Those are just two little "thorns"—two not-so-nice events that can happen. But they can both bring you closer to God. That's how it is with life. Some not-so-nice things are going to happen. But God has said that they can bring us closer to him.

When something not-so-nice happens, you can think, "Oh, there's another thorn. *(Point out a thorn.)* It's not so nice, but it will help make my life a lovely rose *(point out the flower)* for God."

7

Washed by Jesus

Scripture: But you were washed, you were sanctified, you were justified in the name of the Lord Jesus Christ and by the Spirit of our God (1 Cor. 6:11).

Concept: Jesus washes away our sins.

Objects: A pot of dirt, a glass of water, and a small towel

Today we're going to talk about washing. Not washing our clothes but washing ourselves!

How many of you wash your hands before you eat? (Pause for response.) Good! I hope you all do. Our hands should be clean when we eat.

You may be playing outside before you eat, maybe even in the dirt like this. (*Take out the pot of dirt and stick one of your hands into it.*) Your hands get dirty. (*Show them your dirty hand.*) It may not be this bad. Sometimes you can't see that your hands are dirty, but they are.

You shouldn't eat with dirty hands (*indicate the dirt*

again), so an adult says to you, "Go wash your hands."

The dirt doesn't come off all by itself, does it? *(Rub your fingers together a little and show them the still-dirty hand.)*

So you need help. You can't wash dirt away without a little . . . *(show them the glass of water)* . . . water.

There, now we're set. *(With your clean hand, pour half of the water slowly over your dirty hand, rubbing to help the dirt disappear. Put your hand over the pot as you do this so that the water will drip into the pot. Dry your hands and show them your clean hands.)* Nice and clean. I couldn't have done that without water.

You always use water to wash your hands, don't you? That helps get the dirt off, and the idea is to wash away the dirt and keep our bodies clean.

It's the same way with our souls, the part of us that's really us. That's the part of us that God looks at.

God wants us to be clean on the inside. He doesn't like to see sin in our souls. That's like seeing dirt on our hands. *(Stick your hand in the pot of dirt again and show them your hand. Keep the dirty hand in sight for illustration.)* God looks at our souls and says, "There's sin. You don't always obey me. You can't live with me in heaven if you have a dirty soul. Go wash your soul."

Can we get rid of sin all by ourselves? *(Shake your head as you ask the question to encourage the same response.)* It's sort of like this dirt. It sticks and we can't get rid of it. We need some help. We need something to wash away our sins.

Who helps us? Who can wash away our sins? *(Pause for response.)* That's right, Jesus can!

God knew that we wouldn't be able to wash away our sins all by ourselves. But he loved us so much that he sent Jesus to die on the cross for our sins. If we believe that Jesus died for us, our sins don't count. *(Pour water over your dirty hand as you speak.)* They're all washed away. Only Jesus can and does wash away our sins.

The next time you wash your hands, watch the water wash the dirt away. And think of your soul—how it, too, was dirty with sin. Then thank Jesus that he loves you and has washed away all your sins.

8

Someone Special

Scripture: Jesus said, "Let the little children come to me, and do not hinder them, for the kingdom of heaven belongs to such as these" (Matt. 19:14).

Concept: Children are special to Jesus.

Objects: A few pictures of people who are special to you; a mirror

Today I'd like to talk about some special people. *(Show them one of the pictures.)* Does anyone know who this is? *(Pause for response.)* Maybe you don't know; this person may not be special to you. But he [she] is very special to me. This is my [spouse, parent, friend]. This is someone I really love. *(Proceed with a few sentences about the person; for example, why you love him/her, how you spend time together, what you do for each other, and so forth.)*

Here's someone else who's special to me. *(Show them another picture. Continue in this manner until you have shown them all your pictures.)*

I'm sure that you have people who are special to you, too. Your parents, of course; and maybe brothers or sisters, Grandma and Grandpa, aunts and uncles. *(If you feel comfortable with the children and have enough time, you may want to ask them to name some people who are special to them.)* I think everybody has certain people who are special to them.

Now I want to show you someone who is very special to Jesus. *(Take the mirror and hold it so that all of the children can see themselves in it.)* That's right! You are very special to Jesus, and you, and you. *(Point at individual children as you say this.)*

Do you know why you're very special to Jesus? Because you are children! I know, Jesus loves us all, old and young alike, but I think that he loves children especially.

When Jesus lived on earth, he gathered children on his lap. When adults tried to push the children away from him, he stopped the adults. He said that he wanted children to come to him.

Jesus even said that adults should become like children to be able to live with him. Many times, he used children as examples of what people should be like. Jesus especially loved children then, and he still loves children in a special way. So you—each one of you children—is very special to Jesus.

It's nice to have special people in our lives—people like Mom and Dad, or sisters and brothers. It's also nice to know that we are special to them, and they love us very much. But better than all that, it's wonderful to know that you are very special to Jesus.

Look at these special people one more time. *(Let the children see themselves in the mirror again.)* Take a good look, and don't forget: Jesus considers you very special. How can you forget? From now on, every time you look in a mirror and see yourself, you can say, "There's someone that's very special to Jesus!"

9

Shrug It Off

Scripture: "If someone strikes you on the right cheek, turn to him the other also" (Matt. 5:39).

Concept: Shrug off the minor irritations in life.

Object: A picture of a dog or someone washing a dog (*Note:* The picture isn't entirely necessary, especially if you are comfortable with expressive gestures.)

How many of you have a dog at home? (*If you have a picture of a dog, show it now. Pause for response.*) That's great. Aren't dogs good pets?

If you're familiar with dogs, maybe you can tell me this. What does a dog do when it gets wet? Suppose someone gives it a bath, or it gets caught out in the rain. As soon as it's away from that water, what does it do? (*Imitate a dog shaking water from its coat and pause for response.*)

That's right, it shakes itself to shake the water out of its fur [coat].

It doesn't really like to be soaked to the skin. So, the

first chance it gets, it shakes itself *(imitate)* and shrugs off the water. Then it goes on its merry way as if it never got wet. It's easy enough for a dog to get rid of that water.

Can you do that? Pretend for a minute that you're a wet dog, and you want to shrug off the water. What would you do? *(Imitate again, to encourage the children.)*

In a way, Jesus wants us to do just that—shrug it off. He doesn't want us to shake water off ourselves, like a dog. But he does want us to shrug certain things off in our minds.

Have you ever been teased, or had people say not-so-nice things to you? I know I have, and it doesn't feel very nice. I don't like that, just like a dog doesn't like being soaked to the skin. It bothers me, and sometimes I want to say nasty things back.

But Jesus says to forget it. Don't fight back. Turn away from people like that. Shrug it off *(illustrate again)* just like the dog shrugs off the water. Then forget it.

When people aren't nice to you, don't even bother about it. Shrug it off. And turn to Jesus, who will always love you.

10

Love Is Never Out of Style

Scripture: "A new command I give you: Love one another. As I have loved you, so you must love one another" (John 13:34).

Concept: We should love each other all the time.

Objects: Small paper hearts, enough so that each child can have one

I made some "valentines" for you this week. *(Pass out the hearts as you speak.)* Each of you may have one to take home. They're all shaped like hearts to remind us of love. Often when we see hearts, we think of love.

I had to make these myself, because I couldn't find any valentines in the store. Valentine's Day was a long time ago. And it will be a few months before the next Valentine's Day. No one is selling valentines right now.

Some people thought I was a little confused, looking for valentines this time of year. After all, valentines are for Valentine's Day, right? One day a year we send little hearts and say that we love each other. So they thought I was confused, looking for valentines this time of the year.

But I don't think that I'm one bit confused, I know that it's not Valentine's Day. Valentines may be out of style right now, but the heart that I gave you is supposed to remind you of love.

Is love ever out of style? Do we love each other only one day a year? Is Valentine's Day the only day we show people that we love them? *(Pause for response.)* Of course not!

Love is never out of style. Love is in style every day of the year. In fact, God wants us to love each other all the time. And we should show that love all the time.

Jesus told us to love each other, just as he loves us. Does Jesus ever stop loving us? *(Pause for response.)* No! He loves us all the time, every day of every year. And he wants us to love each other the same way. He wants us to love each other all of the time, and he wants us to show that we love each other.

That's why I gave each of you a heart. I just want to tell you that I love you. And I want to remind you that God loves you very much. He wants us all to love each other, all the time.

Take the paper heart home and put it in a place where you will see it. If any of your friends notice it and think that you're mixed up about Valentine's Day, tell them what we talked about. Valentine's Day is only one day in a whole year. But God loves us every day and wants us to show that we love each other every day. This little valentine may be out of style right now, but love is never, never out of style.

11

A Sponge or a Rock?

Scripture: I have hidden your word in my heart that I might not sin against you (Ps. 119:11).

. . . Today, if you hear his voice, do not harden your hearts (Ps. 95:7, 8).

Concept: We should store God's Word in our hearts.

Objects: A sponge, a rock, a glass of water, and a pan

I have two very different things with me today: a sponge and a rock. *(Show them the sponge and the rock.)* The sponge is nice and soft, isn't it? *(Squeeze the sponge a few times to show how soft it is.)* The rock is hard—hard as a rock.

I also have some water here. *(Show them the glass of water.)* I want to pour some of this water out of the glass and use it. Should I pour it onto the rock or the sponge? *(Pause for response.)* Of course, I'll use the sponge!

A rock doesn't soak up any water. Look what happens when I pour water on the rock. *(Put the rock in the pan and pour a little water over it.)* The water runs right off. You can't soak up water with a rock.

But you *can* with a sponge. Watch this. *(Hold the sponge in the palm of your hand and pour a little water on top of it. Keep your hand over the pan to catch the drips.)* I dripped a little; but where is most of the water now? *(Pause for response.)* That's right, it's in the sponge. *(Squeeze the water out of the sponge into the pan.)* A sponge soaks up water really well.

Now pretend that this water *(show them the glass with water left in it)* is God's Word. All the promises that he gives us, all the things that he tells us to do—pretend that they're right here in this glass. God's going to pour out his Word on us; he's going to tell us lots of things and give us many promises. What does he want us to be, sponges or rocks? *(Pause for response.)*

That's right! God wants us to be sponges with his Word. He wants us to remember everything he tells us, and keep his promises in our hearts so that we can live close to him.

God tells us in the Bible that when we hear him speak—when we hear someone read the Bible—we should not harden our hearts. We shouldn't be like this rock. *(Indicate the rock.)* It's too hard; it won't soak up God's Word.

Instead God wants us to say, as it does in the Bible, "I have hidden your word in my heart." God wants us to listen to his Word and remember what he says to us. He wants us to hold his Word in our hearts, just like this sponge *(indicate the sponge)* holds water inside of it.

When we read the Bible in church today [or when your parents read the Bible at home] what are you going to be, a sponge or a rock? God wants you to store up his Word in your heart and remember it. Be a sponge so that you can remember God's promises to you.

12

Applesauce Christians

Scripture: Do not conform any longer to the pattern of this world (Rom. 12:2).

Concept: Don't let the world squeeze you into its mold.

Objects: A container filled with applesauce and an apple

Who can tell me what this is? *(Show the children the applesauce and pause for response. If the children can't guess it right away, comment on the fact that it's rather nondescript, it doesn't look like much.)* You're right! It's applesauce.

Who can tell me where the applesauce comes from? *(Pause for response.)* You're right, it comes from apples. *(Show the children the apple.)* Someone took many apples that looked like this, cut them up, cooked them, mashed them, and turned them into applesauce.

This *(indicate the applesauce)* doesn't look at all like an apple, does it? By looking at it, I wouldn't even be able to see that it came from apples. It may be good, but it's a far cry from apples. It's apples that have been cut up, cooked, and mashed.

I don't really want to talk about apples and apple-sauce this morning. I want to talk about *you*. I want to be sure that you don't become applesauce!

Right now, we could pretend that you're all little apples. Each of you is a whole person, just the way God made you. *(Indicate the apple.)* Each of you is just a little bit different from every one else. [Lisa] is a little different from [Mark]; [Sara] is not at all like [Rachel]. God made each of you a little different. And he loves you just the way you are.

But often people want to change you to be more like they are. And that's not always good. Especially when they want you to do things that God doesn't like.

Have you ever heard someone say, "Come on, everyone is doing it"? Maybe everyone's teasing a certain person. Or everyone is telling little white lies about something, or everyone is cheating at school. People want you to join them, so they say, "Everyone is doing it." That's supposed to make it okay.

But, if you do something just because everyone else is doing it, you're really letting people make you into applesauce. People are changing you, so that you're no different from them. They're trying to make you what *they* want you to be, instead of what *God* wants you to be—making you applesauce instead of apples.

God tells us in the Bible that we shouldn't conform to the pattern of this world. In other words, don't do something just because everybody else is doing it. Instead ask yourself, "Is this what God wants me to do?" That way, you won't become like everyone else—like applesauce.

God loves you just the way he made you. He wants you to be yourself *(indicate the apple)*, an individual apple for him.

13

Be Real

Scripture: Whoever would love life and see good days must keep his tongue from evil and his lips from deceitful speech (1 Peter 3:10).

Concept: God blesses honest people.

Object: An artificial plant

Look at this plant, it's beautiful, isn't it? *(Show the children the plant while you speak.)* The leaves are so green and shiny, and there's not a dead leaf on the stalk. The plant is so full of leaves. It's growing so straight and tall. *(Make any comment applicable to the "plant" that you have.)* This certainly is a gorgeous plant.

But, is it really a plant? Look at it very closely. *(Bring the plant close to the children so that they can examine it and at least a few of them can touch it. Continue to ask questions about the plant as you move it around.)* Feel the leaves if you can. Do they feel like real plant leaves? Not really; they feel a little fake. Is that stalk really a plant stalk or is it just a piece of plastic [or silk]? When you look at it closely, you can see that it's not real. If this were a real plant, would it be so perfect looking? Probably not; real plants usually have a few dead leaves or pieces of leaves on them.

Is this a real plant? *(Pause for response.)* No! It's a fake plant, made to look like a real one. But it can't fool you when you look at it closely.

Now that you know this plant is fake, let me ask you a few questions about it. If you water this "plant" and put it in the sun, will it grow? *(Pause for response.)* Of course not! A fake plant can't grow. Only a real plant can.

Will this plant ever have any flowers? *(Pause for response.)* No! Fake plants can't make flowers; only real plants can do that.

Will this plant ever give me anything to eat? Can it make strawberries, or blueberries, or even tomatoes? *(Pause for response.)* Of course not. Strawberry plants make strawberries and tomato plants give us tomatoes. This plant is neither. It's a fake plant. It won't give us anything, not even another fake plant.

All that this plant can do is sit and try to look like a real plant. It can't make berries or flowers. It can't even grow. It's a fake plant; it's not real.

I think I'd rather have a real plant. Real plants can make flowers and fruit; real plants can grow.

Sometimes I think that people can be a lot like this so-called plant. Sometimes they can be really fake. That sounds strange, doesn't it? Let me explain what I mean.

I think that when people tell lies, they're fakes. They're not telling the truth; they're making something up. They just want to look good, so they tell lies.

Pretend for a minute that you've been playing with a lot of toys. It's time to go to bed, so Mom or Dad asks you to put your toys away. A few minutes later they ask you if your toys are put away. You want to look like you obeyed them, so you say *yes*. That's a lie, isn't it? You are faking it, just because you want to look good for Mom and Dad.

Or suppose you have a fight with a friend of yours. I hope that doesn't happen, but pretend that it does. Someone asks you what is the trouble, and you blame it all on the other person. You know that it's really your fault, too, but you don't want to take the blame. Is that honest? Of course not; you'd be faking it, just to look good.

Do you think God wants us to lie, to be fake people? Absolutely not! God tells us in the Bible that if we want to have a good life, we should watch that we tell the truth, that we're honest and don't tell lies. He warns us not to be fake people.

You see, fake people—people who lie—are a lot like this fake plant. *(Draw their attention to the plant again.)* They may look good, but they can never grow to be good healthy Christians. They can never do really good things for God; they're just plain fake.

God wants you to grow up to be real, beautiful, healthy Christians. He wants to give you good things and watch you grow under his care. He says that he will bless you and be good to you—if you take care to be a good, honest person.

14

God's Road Map to Heaven

Scripture: You have known the holy Scriptures, which are able to make you wise for salvation through faith in Christ Jesus (2 Tim. 3:15).

Concept: The Bible shows us the way to heaven.

Objects: A road map of your city or county and a Bible

Can anyone tell me what this is? *(Show them the map and pause for response.)* That's right, it's a map.

This particular map is a road map. It shows all the roads in [Name]. *(Point out, on the map, certain landmarks with which the children might be familiar. Use the next two paragraphs as a model.)* Here's where our church is. Here's [Kelloggsville] Christian School, and here's [Cutlerville] Christian School.

This map tells me that, to get to [Cutlerville] Christian School from here, I must travel down [Division Avenue, take a left onto Sixty-eighth Street and go east for almost one mile]. *(Trace the routes that you mention.)* If I want to go to [Kelloggsville]

Christian School, I must take [Division to Fifty-second Street]. I do a little curve on [Fifty-second, go almost a mile east,] and I'll be at the school.

If I have this road map in the car with me, and if I use it, I'll never get lost in this city. The road map can give me directions to wherever I want to go.

Road maps are important when you're on a long trip. Road maps show you the way through unfamiliar places and help you get to where you want to go.

God has given each of us a very important road map. His map doesn't show us how to get from church to [Cutlerville] Christian School. It shows us something much more important than that. It shows us how to get from here to heaven!

Can anyone tell me what "road map" I'm talking about? What has God given us that can show us the way to heaven? *(Hold up the Bible while you speak and pause for response.)* That's right. God has given us the Bible. And in the Bible he tells us what we must do to get to heaven and live with him.

God gives us many directions in the Bible. The most important one, of course, is to follow Jesus and believe in him. Then—someday—we will live with him in heaven.

God also maps out our way through life. He tells us that we should honor our parents; that's a good "road" to follow. He says that we should love one another and be kind to each other. That's another good direction for life.

Can anyone think of other directions God has given us for life? *(Pause for answers and add some that aren't given.)* [Doesn't he tell us to pray often? Doesn't he tell us to give to the poor? Doesn't he tell us to praise him?] All these directions are like little streets that we should take while we're traveling to heaven. The main direction, of course, is to follow Jesus.

If you follow God's road map *(hold up the Bible)* to heaven, if you listen to the Bible and follow what God tells you, you will never, never take a wrong turn in life. You can be sure that God will guide you to heaven.

15

Living Water

Scripture: "Whoever drinks the water I give him will never thirst. Indeed, the water I give him will become in him a spring of water welling up to eternal life" (John 4:14).

Concept: Jesus gives us eternal life.

Objects: A potted plant that has gone dry enough for the leaves to droop; a glass of water

This plant looks a little droopy, doesn't it? I've tried to be kind to it. I kept it in sunlight and I even stirred up the soil a bit. Yet it looks like it's about ready to die.

There's one thing I didn't give it, something all plants need. Who can guess what that is? *(Pause for response.)* That's right—water! I haven't watered this plant for a while. It will die if I don't give it water.

(Take the glass of water and water the plant. Leave some water in the glass.) There, that's what it needed. It was dying of thirst. Now it should live.

All plants need water to live. That's why, if we have plants inside our homes, someone must water them.

How many of you have plants in your houses? *(Pause for response.)* I think most of us have some houseplants. Have you ever watched someone water the plants? If you haven't, ask them if you can watch. You'll notice that they water every single plant. That's because every plant needs water to live. A plant that never gets water will die.

Who waters the plants that grow wild? Who waters the grass in the meadows, the wild flowers that grow along the roads, and the trees that grow in the woods? *(Pause for response.)* That's right, God does! God sends rain to water all his plants. When it rains, you can say to yourself, "Look, God is watering his plants."

Water *(hold up the glass with the remaining water in it)* is very, very important. Without water, all plants would die. They simply need water to live.

That's why Jesus called himself living water. Just like plants need water to live, we need Jesus.

Now, we're not plants. And Jesus isn't water, like this water in the glass. That's just a comparison, but it's true. Without Jesus, you cannot live. Your body will live, but your soul, that inside part of you that's really you, cannot live forever without Jesus. Jesus came into the world to die for our sins. And he said that if we believe in him—if we believe that he died for our sins—our souls can live forever with him.

So Jesus called himself living water. If we believe in him, we can live forever with him. Believing in Jesus is like our souls taking a drink of living water.

[*Note:* You may or may not want to include the following concept, depending on the age of the children. If you don't, simply skip the following paragraph.]

There's one big difference between the water in this glass and Jesus, the living water. This plant *(indicate the plant)* will have to be watered again and again. One drink of water won't do it. I have to remember to keep watering my plants or they'll die. But one drink of living water is enough for our souls. Jesus died once for all our sins. And once we truly believe in him, we will live forever with him.

The next time you see someone watering the plants in your house, you'll know they're doing that to keep the plants alive. And the next time it rains, you can remind yourself that God is watering his plants with life-giving water. And that can remind you of Jesus, the only living water for you. Believe in Jesus, and you can live forever with him.

16

Popcorn People

Scripture: We also rejoice in our sufferings, because we know that suffering produces perseverance; perseverance, character; and character, hope (Rom. 5:3, 4).

Concept: Tough times help build our characters.

Objects: A bag of popcorn large enough so that each child can have a handful, a jar of unpopped popcorn

I have a treat for you today. Popcorn! *(Show them the bag of popcorn and pass it out. Continue speaking as you pass it.)* Each of you can have a few pieces but don't eat them yet. I want you to look at them for a little while. You like popcorn, don't you? It's a good snack, healthy and natural. If it pops well, it's so nice and fluffy, ready to melt in your mouth.

Notice I said, "If it pops well." You have to pop popcorn before you can eat it.

Here's some unpopped corn. *(Show them the jar of kernels.)* Could you eat this, just the way it is? *(Pause for response.)* Of course not. These are just popcorn kernels. They're much too tough to eat. *(Shake the jar so they can hear the kernels rattle inside.)* And they don't taste good either. You have to pop these kernels before they're good to eat.

Who can tell me how you pop popcorn? *(Pause for response.)* That's right; you put these kernels in the popcorn popper [or microwave, or a pan on the stove] and heat them. When they become very, very hot, they pop open and become popcorn that you can eat.

Pretend for a minute that you are a popcorn kernel. You don't know what's happening, but someone throws you into a popcorn popper and turns on the heat. Do you think that would be fun? *(Shake your head as you ask the question.)* No! I think you might suffer just a bit in that popper.

Would you complain a bit? *(Nod your head as you ask the question.)* Probably. Especially if you didn't know why the heat was on. Then someone would have to tell you, "It's for your own good. You may be so miserable now, but that heat is going to change you into good popcorn."

I know it's silly to pretend that you're a popcorn kernel. But in a way, we're all like popcorn kernels. Sometimes we need the heat turned on to change us into better people.

Let me explain that a bit.

We all have days that are not-so-good, don't we? Maybe no one wants to play with us. Or a best friend moves away. Or someone lies to us. Or we get a bad grade at school. All those things make for not-so-good days. That's when "the heat's turned on" and we're suffering just a little bit.

The Bible tells us that times like that can make us

into better people. It says that suffering produces character. In other words, you can become a better person, more like God wants you to be, by learning from those not-too-good things that happen.

When no one wants to play, you may learn what it's like to be alone and become a better friend to others. When someone lies to you, you learn how that hurts. Then you remember that God tells us not to tell lies, and you try harder never to tell a lie. If you don't do well at school, you ask God to help you and you learn to try to be the best you can. Through all of those things you ask God to help you become a better person. And gradually you change from a little, hard kernel to a nice, fluffy popcorn. You change into a better, more understanding Christian.

So, the next time something not-so-good happens to you, just think about the popcorn. Maybe the "heat is on" to change you into a better Christian. And remember, there's always someone popping that corn. God is always in control; and he will help you become a better person.

17

Rainbow Promises

Scripture: "Whenever the rainbow appears in the clouds, I will see it and remember the everlasting covenant between God and all living creatures of every kind on the earth" (Gen. 9:16).

Concept: God always keeps his promises.

Object: A picture of a rainbow

I brought a rainbow with me today! It's not a real rainbow. I can't bring a rainbow inside. It's just a picture that I made this week to remind us of rainbows. *(Show them the picture.)* Rainbows are beautiful, aren't they? They're so bright and colorful. I'm always happy when I see a rainbow.

There's a special reason that a rainbow makes me happy. That's because it reminds me that God keeps his promises.

Long ago, after the flood, God promised Noah that he would never again send a flood to destroy the whole world. After he made that promise, God put a rainbow in the sky. And he told Noah that the rainbow was a special reminder of that promise. So every time we see a rainbow, we can remember God's promise not to destroy the world again with a flood.

Have we ever again had a big flood that covered the whole world? *(Pause for response.)* Of course not! God promised that we wouldn't, and God always keeps his promises.

God has given us many promises. Who can tell me some of God's promises? *(Pause for response.)*

[*Note:* The development of this lesson depends on which promises the children mention. After each promise mentioned, reinforce the concepts that: (1) God always keeps his promises, and (2) the rainbow can remind us of that promise. If you are uncomfortable with letting the children develop the lesson, you can follow the examples given below.]

Let me help you a bit. Has God promised that he will always love us? *(Nod your head as you ask the questions.)* Yes, he has! God keeps his promises, so we can be sure that he will always love us. So, when we see a rainbow, we can remember that God will always love us. *(Show them the picture at each mention of the rainbow.)*

Has God promised that he will forgive our sins if we believe in Jesus? Yes! We can be sure that he will, because he has promised, and God always keeps his promises. So a rainbow can remind us that God forgives our sins.

Has God promised that he will always be with us? Yes, he has! We know that God will always be with us, because he promised us that, and God always keeps his promises. So a rainbow can remind us that God is always with us.

Has God promised to take care of us? He has! We

can be sure that God will take care of us, because he promised to do that. When we see a rainbow, we can remember that God will always take care of us.

A rainbow can remind us of many things, can't it? It can remind us that God will always love us, that he will forgive our sins, that he will always be with us, and that he will take care of us [or whatever promises were mentioned]. That's a lot to remember, so let's make it a little easier.

When you see a rainbow outside, you know that God put it there. He wants to remind you that he will always keep his promises to you.

18

God Cares for You

Scripture: And my God will meet all your needs according to his glorious riches in Christ Jesus (Phil. 4:19).

Concept: God cares for us.

Object: A fish in a fishbowl

I brought my pet [gold]fish with me today. It looks rather healthy, doesn't it? That's because I take good care of it.

Do any of you have pet fish? *(Pause for response.)* There are things you have to do to take care of your fish. Do you have to feed it? *(Pause for response.)* Of course! The fish would starve to death if you didn't give it food once in a while.

How about the water in the fishbowl? Do you let it become dirty? *(Pause for response.)* Of course not. Dirty water isn't good for a fish. You have to put clean water in the bowl every once in a while.

And, when you clean the water, do you take the fish

out and put it on the table? *(Pause for response.)* No! A fish can't live out of water. So you put the fish in other water while you put clean water in the fishbowl.

Do you ever put boiling-hot water into the fishbowl? *(Pause for response.)* Of course not! The fish can't live in boiling-hot water, so you carefully put in water that isn't too hot or too cold.

What would happen if you didn't feed your fish, or didn't change its water, or took it out of water, or put it in boiling water? *(Pause for response.)* That's right, the fish would die. That fish depends on you for everything. If you ignore it, or do the wrong things, the fish may die. It belongs to you, so you take good care of it.

[*Note:* If you wish, you can expand the lesson here to include other pets. Ask the children what pets they have. Then lead them, with questions, in a discussion of how they take care of their pets. End each section with mention of the fact that the pet belongs to them, so they take good care of it.]

This fish [or our pets] can tell us something about ourselves. Just like our pets belong to us, we belong to someone too. We're not his pets, but we are his children. Whom do we belong to? *(Pause for response.)* That's right, we belong to God.

And because we belong to God, he loves us very much and he cares for us. He cares for us much better than we care for our pets. The Bible tells us that God will meet all our needs. Jesus told us that God knows what we need even before we ask him, and that God will give us everything we need.

Do you sometimes forget to feed your pet? Maybe an adult must remind you once in a while. But God never, never forgets about us. He's always watching over us and always caring for us.

So the next time you go to feed your pet, stop and think about that for a minute. That pet belongs to you, so you try to take good care of it. You belong to God. And he does take good care of you. He will always love you and will *always* take care of you.

19

Bubbles and Baubles

Scripture: "Do not store up for yourselves treasures on earth, where moth and rust destroy, and where thieves break in and steal. But store up for yourselves treasures in heaven, where moth and rust do not destroy, and where thieves do not break in and steal" (Matt. 6:19, 20).

Concept: We should set our hearts on the things of God.

Objects: A jar of bubble "juice" and a ringer for blowing bubbles

Look what I bought this week. *(Show them the jar of bubble juice.)* It's been a long time since I blew bubbles. I used to love blowing bubbles.

(Blow a few bubbles.) They're beautiful, aren't they? *(Point at a few bubbles.)* Look at that big one, or this tiny one here. Here's a really colorful one.

(Blow a few more bubbles.) The trouble with these bubbles is that they don't last very long. They hit something and pop, or else they just fall apart. *(Pause*

or make a few comments about the bubbles until they're all gone.) Look at that, they've all disappeared already. Bubbles just don't last very long.

But then, not many things last very long. Think about the toys that you had as a young child. Do you still have any of them, or are most of them gone? They're kind of like these bubbles, aren't they? *(Blow a bubble.)* There's your baby toy. *(Pop the bubble.)* It's gone.

That's the way it is with most things; they don't last long. *(Blow another bubble.)* Here's your favorite game. Isn't it fun? *(Pop the bubble.)* Someday it will be broken or lost or worn-out.

(Blow another bubble.) Here's your favorite dress or shoes or jeans. *(Pop the bubble.)* By next year, it will probably be gone, worn-out, or too small.

Here's your favorite book. *(Blow another bubble and pop it right away.)* Oops! You lost it, or ripped a page. It's gone.

Here's your bike. *(Blow another bubble.)* You left it out in the rain and it became rusty. Someday it will fall apart. *(Pop the bubble.)*

But we didn't come here to talk about bubbles and things that fall apart. Instead, let's talk about things that last forever.

What can you think of that will last forever? *(Pause for response.)* That's right, God [or Jesus]! Only God and his promises and his Word will last forever. His promises will never wear out or fail. You will never lose God or outgrow him. He's the only thing in your life that will last forever.

Jesus talked about this. He told us not to set our minds on (or become all wrapped up in) the things of this world. They won't last forever, and they will disappoint us. Instead, he said, set your mind on God and his Word. Then you will never be disappointed because he will always be here for you.

Bubbles are fun. *(Blow a few more bubbles.)* Toys and games are fun, but they won't last. So set your mind and hopes on God and his promises. They will never disappear like these bubbles did. God with his love and promises will last forever.

20

Grow in the Lord (1)

Scripture: But grow in the grace and knowledge of our Lord and Savior Jesus Christ (2 Peter 3:18).

Concept: We should make a conscious effort to grow in the Christian faith.

Objects: A few packets of flower seeds (be sure there are enough seeds so that each child can take some home)

I've brought some flower seeds with me today. I love pretty flowers, don't you? *(Pause for response.)* Good! I brought enough seeds for all of us. I thought that if we all kept some seeds, pretty soon we could all have some flowers. Would you like that? Good! Then I'll give you each some seeds. *(Pass out the seeds.)* Now all we have to do is sit and wait for them to grow.

Wait a minute! Do you think these seeds will grow into healthy plants with beautiful flowers if we do nothing for them? *(Pause for response.)* Of course not!

What should we do to these seeds? *(Pause for response. How you proceed depends on the responses. Suggestions are given below.)*

That's right, we should plant them. We should put them in little pots full of dirt and cover them up with soil. Seeds usually can't grow unless they're planted.

What else should we do for our seeds? *(Pause for response.)* Of course; after we plant them, we should water them. It won't do any good to plant them and then forget them. They need water to grow.

Can you think of anything else? *(Pause for response.)* That's a good idea. We should make sure that they get some sun. Plants are usually healthier if they grow in the sun.

Look at your seeds for a minute. They're neat little things, aren't they? They don't look like much right now, but we know that they can grow into healthy plants with beautiful flowers. But they won't grow without a little care. And, probably, the more care we give our seeds, the better they'll grow.

In a way, you can think of yourself as a seed. I know, you don't look like a seed, and you're not going to grow up to be a plant. But if you love Jesus, you're a very special kind of seed; you're a Christian seed! You can grow up to be a fine, healthy Christian.

But Christians need care and tending, just like these seeds need care to grow into healthy plants. Fine, strong Christians who love Jesus and work for him don't just happen. They grow with a lot of care and a lot of help from God.

Who can tell me one thing you can do to care for your Christian life? *(Pause for response. How you proceed depends on suggestions given by the children. Examples are given below.)*

That's right, you can pray a lot. God wants you to talk to him and stay close to him. He wants to help you grow, but you must ask him to help you.

The Bible is also very important. That's God's Word to you. You could almost think of it as instructions for growing. It's important to know what God says to you, what's in the Bible, if you want to grow as a Christian. So it's important to listen well when someone reads the Bible.

When you know what God wants you to do, then what? Should you just say, "Oh, that's nice!" or should you try to follow instructions? *(Pause for response.)* Yes, it's very important to try to do what God tells us to do.

So, now you have at least three things that you can do to grow as a Christian. You can read your Bible, you can pray often to stay close to God, and you can try to live as God wants you to live. If you do those things, you'll be caring for your Christian life. It takes care to grow as a Christian, just like it takes care for these seeds to grow into healthy plants.

I'd like you to try something for me. Take your seeds home and plant them. Make sure that you take care of them. Try to grow a few plants.

As you're taking care of these seeds, you can remind yourself that you also need care as a Christian. You can remember to read the Bible, pray often, and try to do what God wants you to do.

Maybe in a few months we can see how our seeds—and our Christian lives—are growing.

21

Make a Joyful Noise

Scripture: Come, let us sing for joy to the LORD; let us shout aloud to the Rock of our salvation (Ps. 95:1).

Concept: Sometimes it's good to shout and sing and make a joyful noise to the Lord.

Object: Nothing

I didn't bring anything to show you today, because I want to talk about something that you can't see. But you can hear it; it's your voice.

You don't use your voice in church very often, do you? *(Shake your head as you speak to elicit a similar response.)* In fact if you start talking, an adult will be quite quick to tell you to be quiet.

I want to change all that for a few minutes. While you're up here today, I want you to use your voice, okay? We'll call it a practice for something that you should do once in a while.

You see, the Bible tells us to use our voices in all sorts of ways to praise God. Sometimes we forget that it's good to make a joyful noise to God.

The Bible says that we should proclaim aloud God's praise (Ps. 26:7). That means we should praise him—aloud—with our voices, like this: **Praise the Lord.** Let's not be shy; let's praise the Lord together. Can you praise the Lord with me? *(Give the children a visual cue with your hand.)* Praise the Lord! Let's do it again, a little louder: *Praise the Lord,* **Praise the Lord!** Maybe we should do that more often—praise the Lord aloud.

The Bible also says that we should shout to God with cries of joy (Ps. 47:1). *Hallelujah* is a good shout of joy. *(You may be more comfortable substituting Amen for Hallelujah.)* Maybe once in a while we should shout *Hallelujah!* Can you shout for joy with me? *(Give the children a visual cue again.)* Hallelujah! *Hallelujah!* **Hallelujah!**

The Bible also talks about clapping our hands as we shout to God. That's a really joyful way to praise the Lord. *Hallelujah, Praise the Lord! (Clap as you shout for joy.)* Join me; shout and clap! *Hallelujah, Praise the Lord!* **Hallelujah, Praise the Lord!**

What else can we do with our voices? *(Pause for response.)* That's right, we can sing! The Bible often talks about singing with joy before the Lord. And we do sing in church. We'll have a chance to sing with everyone else in just a little while. I don't think we have to practice that now.

But I do think that we often need more practice for praising the Lord aloud and shouting for joy. Sometimes we forget that God doesn't want us to be silent about all the good things he does for us. He wants us to praise him a lot and very loudly.

So praise the Lord aloud with me one more time:

Praise the Lord! And let's shout for joy one more time: *Hallelujah!*

Now, when you go back to your seat, Mom and Dad will probably want you to be quiet, except while we're singing. But don't forget what we practiced. And don't forget that God wants us to make a joyful noise to him.

So the next time you're playing with friends and having a good time, throw in a happy *Hallelujah!* or *Praise the Lord!* Let people know that you're happy and that you want to make a joyful noise to the Lord.

22

Don't Get Hooked

Scripture: Satan himself masquerades as an angel of light (2 Cor. 11:14).

Concept: Sin can be very tempting.

Objects: A fishhook and an artificial worm

How many of you have ever gone fishing? *(Pause for response.)* Even if you haven't, I'll bet you can tell me what this is. *(Show them the hook.)* That's right, it's a fishhook. It's a nasty little thing, so I won't pass it around. I don't want anyone to get hooked.

When we go fishing, we throw this hook into the water and hope that a fish bites on it. It will get caught in the fish's mouth, and we can reel the fish in.

But fish won't bite on a nasty little fish hook. They're smart enough to know that this hook isn't food, so they'll simply swim away from it and find some good food.

To fool the fish, we have to cover up this hook so that they can't see it. *(Take out the artificial worm and put it on the hook.)* There! Now you can't see the hook.

(Show the children the worm with the hook hidden inside.) Now maybe someone can catch a fish with this. Anyone who fishes knows that the hook must be covered with something that will tempt the fish to bite it.

Satan knows that it's the same way with us. *(While you are speaking, take the worm off the hook.)* Satan likes to go fishing for God's people. He wants to make us sin by doing things that God doesn't want us to do. That way he can hook us and drag us away from God. *(Make a hooking and dragging motion in the air with the empty hook.)*

But he knows that Christians try to avoid sin. So Satan makes sin look tempting. He helps us think of all sorts of excuses why we should do something that God doesn't want us to do. *(Slowly put the worm back on the hook while you speak.)*

Maybe you've heard some of these excuses: God won't care. Everybody's doing it. Just this once. Don't be such a goody-goody. Try it; you'll like it. Those excuses are like worms on hooks. They're just excuses to cover up a sin. They're usually just reasons someone will give us to do something God doesn't want us to do.

[*Note:* If you have the time and courage, you can ask the children to supply you with some "worms" by telling you excuses people give to cover up sin.]

Don't get hooked. When you're tempted to do something wrong, don't let all those excuses fool you. Think of this worm. *(Show them the hook with the worm on it.)* There's a nasty little hook beneath it. Then ask yourself, "What does God want me to do?" That way you can stay close to God, and Satan won't catch you when he goes fishing.

23

Life in the Son

Scripture: He who has the Son has life; he who does not have the Son of God does not have life (1 John 5:12).

Concept: Belief in Jesus is absolutely necessary for eternal life.

Object: The sun (*Note:* Take along a picture of the sun in case it isn't shining during the object lesson. If it is shining, you could have the children sit in the sunlight.)

I had you sit in this little patch of sunlight today because I want to talk about the sun for a little while. [Or: Who can tell me what this is? Of course, it's a picture of the sun. Since the sun isn't out today, a picture will have to do.]

It's nice to have the sun out, isn't it? We feel warm and cozy sitting in the sunlight. I'm always happy to see the sun.

Who can tell me some nice things about the sun? What does the sun give us? *(Pause for response. How you proceed depends on the responses. Try to lead the chil-*

dren to mention heat and light from the sun, as follows.) That's right, the sun helps plants grow. Yes, the sun gives us daylight. How about heat? Is sunlight warm or cold? It's warm, isn't it? The sun gives us warmth. If it weren't for the sun, earth would be a cold place to live. What else does the sun give us? What about light? That's right, the sun gives us light. Without the sun our days would be as dark as our nights. Would you like to live in a place that was always dark as night? *(Pause for response.)* Of course not. The sun is very important to us; it gives us light and heat that we need.

In fact the sun is so important that we couldn't live without it. Plants need sunlight to grow. If God didn't give us sunlight, we wouldn't be able to grow any food.

And if the sun never shone, it would be too cold to live here. It would be colder than the coldest day you've ever felt. You would have to put on all your heavy jackets and coats, and still it would be too cold for you to move outside.

When God created everything, he put the sun in just the right place so that we can live here. He knew that we must have sunlight and heat from the sun to live. So, when you see the sun, you can thank God that he put it right where he did in the sky.

Lots of people like to compare Jesus to the sun. Do they mean that Jesus is a big ball of light up in the sky? Of course not. They mean that Jesus is as important to us as the sun is. In fact, Jesus is more important to us than the sun. Let me explain that.

The Bible tells us that Jesus came to save us from our sins. If we believe that Jesus is God, and if we love him because he came to save us, someday we can live forever in heaven with him. How many of you love Jesus? *(Pause for response.)* Good! If you love Jesus and believe that he is God, someday you can live forever in heaven with him.

Some people don't love Jesus. They don't believe that he is God. The Bible tells us that people who don't love Jesus cannot live forever in heaven with him.

So Jesus is very, very important to us. He gives us eternal life in heaven with him. Without Jesus, we don't have life in heaven. With Jesus, we do.

That's sort of like the sun, isn't it? Because God put the sun in the sky, we get everything we need to live on earth. And because God sent his son, Jesus, and we love him, we will be able to live with him in heaven.

So when you see the sun, it can remind you of Jesus. You can think of how important the sun is for life on earth. And then you can remember that Jesus, the Son of God, is all-important to us. He gives us eternal life with him in heaven.

24

God Looks Inside

Scripture: "Man looks at the outward appearance, but the LORD looks at the heart" (1 Sam. 16:7).

Concept: God looks at our hearts, not our physical appearances.

Object: A bag of peanuts in the shells, enough so that each child can have a few

Look what I brought with me today, a bag of peanuts! *(Hold up the bag so that all the children can see the peanuts.)* Do you like peanuts? *(Pause for response.)* Good! I do, too; and I've brought enough so that we all can have some. *(Pass out the peanuts, but continue to talk as you do so.)*

Let's not eat the peanuts now. Let's not even crack them open. We'll make a mess up here if we do. Instead, let's just hold our peanuts and look at them for a little while. These are yours to keep. You may take them home after church today. Then maybe someone can help you crack them open. Just leave them in the shell for now.

Look at your peanuts in the shells. They're really not very pretty, are they? They're a rather dull color, just a light tan. They're all lumpy. Some are two little lumps, and some are just one. The shells themselves have funny little bumps and grooves in them. I don't know why; that's just the way God made them. And they look so dry. Who would ever think that there are good little peanuts inside of them?

Shake your peanuts just a little bit. Can you hear them rattle around inside the shell? That's the only way you know that they're there. You can't see them, yet you know that if you crack one of those funny-looking shells open, there will be a delicious peanut inside.

Besides tasting so good, peanuts are good for you. The shells aren't, of course. But the little peanuts inside the shells have lots of things to keep you healthy and growing well.

No one would know, just by looking at a peanut, that it's such a good thing to eat. Look at your peanuts again. Do they look like they're good to eat? *(Pause for response.)* Of course not! But you know what's inside, so you forget about the shell and you think of those good little peanuts, and most of you say, "I love peanuts."

I had you look at your peanuts—really, at the peanut shells—and think about the good little nuts inside for a special reason. I want you to think about the way God looks at you.

You see, God looks at you just like you look at your peanuts. You don't really care that the peanuts shells are dull and dry and bumpy, do you? You think about that good little peanut inside, so you don't care at all about the shell. God doesn't care what you look like either. He doesn't care if you're good-looking or as plain as a peanut, although no one looks like a peanut. He doesn't care what kind of clothes you wear or how you comb your hair. That's just part of your "shell" and that makes no difference to him.

The Bible says that God looks at your heart. He looks right past your "shell." He cares about what you think and how you feel and if you love him. He knows what's inside of you, and that's what's important.

What matters to God is if you love him and want to please him. God loves you because of what you are inside, not because of what you look like outside. Just like you love peanuts because the little nuts taste so good; the shell makes absolutely no difference.

You may take your peanuts back to your seats with you, but don't crack them open and eat them yet. *(Emphasize this, as some child may be allergic to peanuts.)* Wait until you get home; then an adult can help you. But you may look at your peanuts every once in a while. When you do, think about those good little nuts inside the funny shells. And then you can remember that God doesn't look at your "shell." He loves you for what you have inside.

25

Be Happy!

Scripture: Rejoice in the LORD and be glad, you righteous; sing, all you who are upright in heart! (Ps. 32:11).

Concept: Be happy, God loves you!

Object: A happy face big enough for all the children to see

How many of you have seen one of these? *(Show them the happy face and pause for response.)* That's what I thought, almost everyone. Who can tell me what it's called? *(Pause for response.)* That's right, it's a happy face.

People often draw happy faces on letters or on signs, just to spread a little cheer. All a happy face means is "Be happy!" Isn't that a pleasant thought?

Sometimes I think that maybe there aren't enough happy faces around. I still see a lot of dull, grumpy people.

But then maybe the problem is that people don't know what to be happy about. When someone draws a happy face and tells you to be happy, maybe they'd better give you a reason.

I've got the perfect reason for a happy face; it should make us smile every time. This happy face, instead of just saying "Be happy," says "Be happy, God loves you!" Now that should make everyone smile.

God has said in the Bible that he loves us. And he's promised to be with us always. And he's told us that if we love Jesus, we will live forever with him, and we will be forever happy.

Sure, sometimes not-too-nice things happen to us. But God has promised to stay close to us and take care of us through all those times. So if you love God, you can smile through even the not-too-nice times.

Christians should be the happiest people in the world, don't you think so? *(Pause for response.)* Of course!

Yet, Christians often walk around with long faces *(demonstrate)* just like other people. There's no need for that. We know that Jesus loves us and has saved us, so we can always smile. *(Change your frown to a smile.)*

So this is just a little reminder. *(Show them the happy face again.)* When you see one of these—and even when you don't—you can smile and say, "I'm happy; God loves me!"

26

The Perfect Hiding Place

Scripture: You are my hiding place; you will protect me from trouble and surround me with songs of deliverance (Ps. 32:7).

Concept: God is our hiding place in times of trouble.

Object: A turtle or a picture of one

Who can tell me what this is? *(Show them the turtle or the picture and pause for response.)* That's right, it's a turtle.

One neat thing about a turtle is that it carries its protection, its own little hiding place, right on its back.

[If you have a picture] Pretend for a minute that this turtle is minding its own business, walking through the woods. Then someone comes along and bothers it. Maybe a boy pokes a stick at it. Or an animal comes and wants to take a bite out of it. What would the turtle do? *(Pause for response.)* That's right. The turtle simply pulls itself into its shell. Then it's hiding and is protected from danger.

[If you have a turtle: put the turtle on the floor and let it walk a bit. Talk about it while it gathers courage.] This turtle may stay in its shell because it thinks that I am dangerous. But if it does walk, we can watch what it does when it feels like it is in danger. There it goes! Now, I'm going to make it think that I am danger. *(When the turtle starts to walk, bother it a bit so that it draws back into its shell.)* I'll bother it just a little bit. What does it do right away? Of course, it pulls back into its shell; then it's hiding and is protected from danger.

The turtle is really fortunate, isn't it? It always has a hiding place handy. It carries its protection wherever it goes.

Wouldn't you love to have a hiding place like that all the time? Wouldn't you love to have some protection with you wherever you go? *(Pause for response.)* Then, whenever you felt like you were in danger, or whenever things really bothered you, you could simply pull up into your "shell."

You *do* have a hiding place like that! You *do* have protection with you all the time! Of course, it's not just a little shell. It's much better than that.

Who can tell me what your hiding place, your protection, is? *(Pause for response.)* Of course, it's God!

The Bible says that God is our hiding place; God will protect us from trouble.

When things aren't going too well, or when you just want to get away from it all, you can go to God in prayer. Or when it seems like there's trouble all around you, you can ask Jesus to be with you and to protect you.

Of course, people won't see you disappear. But God isn't a shell. He's much better than a shell; he's God! And he has promised that he will always surround you and protect you. Whenever you call on him, he will be right there.

I've always thought that a turtle shell would be a really neat thing to have. *(Show them the turtle or the picture again.)* But we have something much better for our hiding place and protection. We have God. This turtle is only a small reminder of our perfect hiding place.

27

Grow in the Lord (2)

Scripture: But grow in the grace and knowledge of our Lord and Savior Jesus Christ (2 Peter 3:18).

Theme: To grow as a Christian requires conscious effort.

Objects: A small plant growing in a clay pot and a Bible (*Note:* Ideally, this should be a seedling from the seeds used in "Grow in the Lord (1)." Provision is made for the use of that particular seedling or any other small plant.)

W ho can tell me what this is? (*Show them the seedlings and pause for response.*) That's right, it's a little plant growing in a pot. That's easy to see. I was hoping that this little plant would remind you of something.

Let me give you a hint. Several weeks ago I gave all of you some flower seeds. Who remembers that? (*Pause for response.*) I asked you to do something with those seeds. Do you remember what I asked you to do? (*Pause for response.*) That's right, I asked you to plant the seeds. Who did plant those seeds? *(Raise your hand as you ask the question.)* Good! Some of you did. Do you have little plants growing now? *(Pause for response.)* That's great; we have several little plants growing. I planted my seeds, too. This is what I have now. *(Indicate the pot with the seedlings.)*

[*If you're using different seedlings, skip the last two sentences and use the following instead.*] My seeds didn't grow too well; I must have done something wrong. I had to find another little plant to remind you of the seeds we talked about. This plant looks like it's growing well, so we'll have to pretend that it grew from the seeds I planted.

Who can tell me what we have to do to make seeds grow into healthy, little plants like this? We talked about this when I gave you the seeds. Who remembers? *(Pause for response.)*

That's right, we said we have to care for the seeds. We have to plant them, water them, and make sure they get some sunlight.

I think I took fairly good care of these seeds [or little plants]. They seem to be doing well. It took a little work on my part, but they're still growing. How many of you remembered to do those things for your seeds? *(Pause for response.)*

When I gave you those seeds, we weren't really talking only about little seeds and plants. I gave you those seeds to remind you of something. Do you remember that I said that you were like the seeds I gave you?

I called you little Christian seeds. I said that if you believe in Jesus, you're just like little Christian seeds. You're not grown up yet, but you have everything you need to be a strong, healthy Christian. But just like you

81

had to take care of your seeds, you also have to take care that you grow as a Christian. There were some things that I asked you to do. Does anyone remember one of them?

Let me give you a hint. *(Show them the Bible.)* What did we say about the Bible? *(Pause for response.)* That's right, we should read our Bibles. The Bible is God's Word to us. If we want to be strong Christians, we should know what God says to us. We should listen carefully when someone reads the Bible, God's Word, to us. How many of you have remembered to learn your Bible stories and listen carefully when God's Word is read? *(Raise your hand as you ask the question, and pause for response.)* That helps you grow to be a strong Christian.

What else helps you grow as a Christian? Let me give you another hint. *(Fold your hands and close your eyes as if you are praying.)* That's right, prayer! Besides listening to God's Word, we should talk to God in prayer every day. That way we can stay close to God and grow strong in him. How many of you remember to talk to God in prayer every day? *(Raise your hand as you ask the question and pause for response.)*

There's one more thing that you should do to grow as a Christian. I don't have a hint for this one. Does anyone remember what we said? *(Pause for response.)* Should we do whatever we want to do, or should we try to do what God wants us to do? *(Pause for response.)* That's right. We should try to do what God wants us to do.

God wants us to grow into strong, healthy Christians. He's told us certain things that we should and should not do, to grow well and to please him. He wants us to be kind and generous to people, he wants us to love people; and, above all, he wants us to love him. If we love him, we'll do what he wants us to do.

So again, these are the things that you should do to grow into a strong, healthy Christian. Can you tell me what they are, one more time? *(Pause for response.)* That's right: You should pray to God, you should know the Bible, and you should try to do what God wants you to do.

Everybody needs care to grow as a Christian, just as this little plant needs care if it is to become a big plant. *(Indicate the seedling.)* This plant is growing. It's much bigger than the little seed that was planted several weeks ago. You're growing as Christians, too. Every day you grow just a little bit, just like this plant. But you have to remember to take care of your Christian life, just like we have to take care of the plants that we grow.

28

God's Temples

Scripture: Don't you know that you yourselves are God's temple and that God's Spirit lives in you? . . . God's temple is sacred, and you are that temple (1 Cor. 3:16, 17).

Concept: We should care for our bodies because they are God's temples.

Objects: Your church building and the children

I brought nothing to show you today because it's already here! I want you to look at the church. You can stand up, but stay right where you are. Look around a little bit. And while you look around, ask yourself a question: Is this church dirty and messy or is it neat and clean?

Look at the aisles where people walk down to go to their seats. Are they dirty with all sorts of trash in them? *(Pause for response.)* No! They're very neat and clean.

Now look at the windows. Are they broken and

dirty, or do they look neat and clean? *(Pause for response.)* They're neat and clean too.

Look at this communion table. *(Indicate the proper table.)* Does it have a lot of junk on it, or is it neat and clean? *(Pause for response.)* Of course, it's neat and clean.

How about this pulpit? *(Indicate the pulpit.)* Messy and dirty or neat and clean? *(Pause for response.)* It's neat and clean, isn't it? It may have things that the minister needs to use this morning; that's what pulpits are for. But everything is arranged neatly, and it's all clean.

(Continue this as long as you please, indicating a neat, clean church.)

You may sit down quietly again and face me.

We like to have a neat, clean church. After all, whom do we worship in this church? *(Pause for response.)* That's right, we worship God here. Sometimes we even call this church "God's house." Out of respect for God, because we love him and want to honor him, we keep our church neat and clean. We keep God's house neat and clean.

But God doesn't really live here, does he? We worship him here, but he goes with us when we leave this church.

God doesn't live in this church because he has a far better home. God lives in *you!* He lives in you *(point at each of the children),* and you, and you, and you. Did you know that God's Spirit lives in you?

The Bible says that you are God's temple—that's like his church—and that the Spirit of God lives in *you.*

Look at yourself: your arms, your legs, your body. God is living in that body.

Now, if we keep our church neat and clean because

we worship God here, how should we keep our bodies, God's temples? *(Pause for response.)* That's right, we should keep our bodies neat and clean. We should take good care of our bodies and treat them with respect, because God's Spirit lives in us.

What can we do to take good care of our bodies, God's temples? *(Pause for response. Call on one of the children. How you proceed depends on the answer.)*

[*Note:* If you are not comfortable with that, you can prompt the children with questions such as, "Should we eat foods that are good for us?" and proceed. Depending on your situation, you may want to mention drugs, smoking, liquor, and so forth.]

Yes, we should eat foods that are good for us. Adults who take care of us know what's good for us to eat. They can help us with that. To keep our bodies healthy for God, we can eat the right foods.

We should put only good things into our bodies, right? We don't want a lot of junk in God's temples. We'll stay away from the things that are not good for us and put only good food into our bodies.

That's right, getting enough sleep helps, too. Sometimes we don't want to go to bed on time. But God made our bodies to need rest. And since our bodies are God's temples, we should take care of them and get enough rest.

We should keep ourselves neat and clean. We keep this church neat and clean. But since the Spirit of God really lives in us, we should also keep ourselves neat and clean.

I think that you get the idea. We keep this church neat and clean because we worship God here. But our bodies are God's temple, where God lives, so we should take good care of them.

Now every time you come to church and see it so neat and clean, you can remember that we worship God here. But that happens only on Sunday. Yet whenever you take a bath or shower, or brush your teeth, or eat your vegetables, you can know that you are taking care of your body, God's temple, because God is always with you and his Spirit lives right in you.

29

Known by Your Fruits

Scripture: "By their fruit you will recognize them" (Matt. 7:16).

Concept: We are known by what we do.

Objects: Two pictures of trees, an orange, an apple

Who can tell me what kind of tree this is? *(Show them one of the pictures and pause for response.)* It's a little hard to tell. We know that it's a tree, but we'd have to guess at exactly what kind of tree it is.

Suppose I told you that I picked this *(show them the apple)* from the tree. Now could you tell me what kind of tree it is? *(Pause for response.)* Of course, it's an apple tree!

What kind of tree is this? *(Show them the second picture and pause for response.)* Again, it's hard to tell. It could be one of dozens of kinds of trees. It could be an apple tree; it looks a lot like the other picture. But then, maybe it isn't.

Pretend that I picked this *(show them the orange)* from that tree. What kind of tree is it? *(Pause for response.)*

Correct, it's an orange tree. You probably knew that as soon as you saw the orange.

You couldn't tell what kind of trees these were without the fruit. But you know that an apple comes from the apple tree and an orange comes from an orange tree. You know what kind of trees they are by the fruit that they bear.

Jesus said that it's the same way with people. He said, "By their fruit you will recognize them."

Of course, he didn't mean that people sprout apples and oranges. By "fruit" Jesus meant what people do. You can know what a person is like by watching what that person does. By their fruit (or what they do) you shall know them.

Jesus also said that good trees bring forth good fruit and bad trees bring forth bad fruit. Again he was talking about people. Can anyone tell me what he meant when he said that? *(Pause for response.)* That's right! Jesus meant that bad people do bad things and good people do good things. You know that a person is good if that person does good things.

Did you ever think of yourself as a tree? That sounds strange, but you are a tree in the way that Jesus was talking. You do things—for people, to people, with people—every day. That means you bear fruit every day.

So now the question is, what kind of fruit do you bear? Do you do good things? Do you do the type of things that Jesus wants you to do? Do you love people? Do you share with others? Do you treat people with respect? Do you show Jesus' love? That's bearing good fruit. Jesus said that we would be known by our fruit. People should know by the way we act that we love Jesus. Jesus wants us all to bear good fruit—to do good things—for him.

30

The Trinity

Scripture: ". . . in the name of the Father and of the Son and of the Holy Spirit" (Matt. 28:19).

Concept: God exists in three persons—as the Father, the Son, and the Holy Spirit.

Objects: A glass with ice cubes and water in it (*Note:* If you fill the glass with ice cubes about three hours before this object lesson, some of the ice should be nicely melted down to water.)

I've brought a glass of ice with me today. *(Show them the glass.)* Well, it was all ice when I put it into this glass. A few hours ago I filled the glass with ice cubes. Now some of them have melted, so we have some ice and some water.

Who can tell me what an ice cube is made of? *(Pause for response.)* That's right, ice is frozen water. When we make ice cubes, we put water in little trays in our freezers. Then the water freezes and becomes ice.

So I really just have a glass of water here, don't I? I've got frozen water called ice and I've got liquid water just called "water." It's water in two different forms, but it's all water.

Water comes in a third form, too. Can anyone tell me what that is? Let me give you a hint. When I boil water really fast on the stove, I can see a foggy, little mist above the pan. What's that called? It's SSSSS_____. (Pause for response.) That's right, it's called "steam."

When we boil water, we get steam. Steam is just boiled water that goes up into the air. You can't see it very well, not nearly as well as you can see these ice cubes or this water, but it's there. Steam is just boiled water.

So we can have our water in three different forms. We can freeze it for ice, we can drink it as liquid water, and we can boil it for steam. It's all the same water in three different forms.

In a strange sort of way, this water can remind us of God. Let me explain what I mean.

How many of you have heard of Jesus? (Pause for response.) Good, all of you. You know that Jesus came to save us from our sins. Jesus can save us because he's very special. He's not an ordinary man. (Shake your head to elicit the proper response.) No! Jesus is special and he can save us because he is God; We can call him Jesus or we can call him God. Jesus is God.

How many of you have heard this? "Our Father, who art in heaven"? (Pause for response.) Of course, that's often the way we begin our prayers. Whom are we praying to? That's right, we're praying to God. We call him "our Father in heaven."

We know that Jesus is God and we know that our Father in heaven is God. That's sort of like water and ice. They're both the same God—there is only one God—yet there's Jesus and there's the Father.

How many of you have heard of the Holy Spirit? *(Pause for response.)* The Holy Spirit works in our hearts. We can't see him, but we can feel him working when we love God and want to please him. The Holy Spirit is very real and works inside of every Christian. The Holy Spirit is God, too, just like Jesus and the Father are God. The Holy Spirit is another form of God, just like steam is another form of water.

There's only one God, but he shows himself to us in three different ways; as Jesus the Son, as the Father, and as the Holy Spirit. That's hard to understand, isn't it? It's hard for adults to understand, too.

That's why I thought that this water might help you. When you see water or ice or steam, you can know that it's all water, just three different forms. And you can remember that Jesus, our Father in heaven, and the Holy Spirit are all our one loving God.

31

Praise the Lord!

Scripture: Let everything that has breath praise the LORD. Praise the LORD (Ps. 150:6).

Concept: Praise the Lord!

Objects: Any series of natural objects or pictures of them will do. Exactly what you will say depends on what you have. A picture of sun, moon, and stars, one of trees, and one of animals are used below.

C an everybody see this picture? *(Hold up the picture of sun, moon, and stars.)* What is it? *(Pause for response.)* Right, it's a picture of the sun and the moon and the stars. Who made the sun, moon, and stars? *(Pause for response.)* Of course, God made them. Every time we see the sun or moon or stars, we can remember that God made them and put them in the sky. We can praise God for making the sun, moon, and stars just the way he did.

(Repeat the above procedure for every picture or object that you have: What is this? Who made it? Every time

93

we see it we can remember that God made it. We can praise God for making it just the way he did.)

Did you notice something I said after each picture? I said, "Every time we see it we can remember that God made it, and then we can . . ." *(Pause for response.)* That's right, we can praise God!

The Bible talks a lot about praising God. It says that the sun and moon and stars should praise God. It says that fruitful trees should praise God. It says that everything that has life should praise God.

I'm not sure how the sun, moon, and stars, or how trees and animals praise God. But I know they can remind us to praise him. Every time we see them we can think, "God made them. Praise the Lord!"

There are all sorts of ways that we can praise the Lord. Can anyone tell me one? *(Pause for response. How you proceed depends on what the children contribute. If you feel uncomfortable with that you can prompt them with questions such as,* "Can we sing to praise God?") That's right, we can sing God's praises. We do that in church. But we can also sing anytime. We can sing praise to God.

What else can we do? How about shouting? We can shout praise to God, can't we? We can shout, *"Praise the Lord!"*

Can we dance in praise to the Lord? Of course! Do you ever feel so happy that you just want to move around and dance? We can get up and swing our arms and dance and say, "Praise the Lord!" *(If you feel comfortable with this, you can have the children do a short "dance," saying,* "Praise the Lord!") Some people lift their hands in praise to God. They go like this. *(Demonstrate.)* Shall we lift our hands in praise to the Lord? *(Have the children do it with you.)*

You can probably think of other ways to praise the Lord too. There are all sorts of people in the world with all sorts of ways to praise God. The important thing is that we never forget to praise God in any way that we can think of.

Are you happy? Do you love Jesus? Are you glad that God made you, and that he made the world and everything in it? Then praise the Lord!

You probably don't need anything to remind you to praise God, do you? But if you do, just look around you at all the good things he's made: the sun, the moon, the stars, trees, animals, birds [and so forth]. Anytime you see any of those you can think, "God made them. God made everything. God made me and loves me." And then you can praise the Lord.

32

God's Favorites

Scripture: There is neither Jew nor Greek, slave nor free, male nor female, for you are all one in Christ Jesus (Gal. 3:28).

Concept: God has no favorites; we are all equal in Christ.

Objects: A fruit basket or other container holding various fruits

Look at the fruit basket I received this week. Isn't it beautiful? There are so many different kinds of fruit here, I hardly know which one to eat first. I see several of my favorites.

Look at this orange. *(Hold up an orange.)* It looks delicious! Oranges are one of my favorite fruits. They're so juicy and sweet. And they have lots of vitamins that are good for me. So I always feel good about eating oranges. And I eat a lot of oranges because I like them so much. How many of you like oranges? *(Pause for response.)* Great! How many of you think oranges are your favorite fruit? *(Pause for response.)*

But there are other good fruits in here. Look at these bananas. *(Hold up the bananas.)* Sometimes I think I like bananas almost better than oranges. They're not as juicy, but they're so easy to peel and eat. And they're good for me too. They don't have the same vitamins as oranges do, but they have other good things in them. I eat quite a few bananas too. How many of you like bananas? *(Pause for response.)* Are they your favorite fruit?

Here are some grapes. *(Hold up a bunch of grapes.)* I love to eat grapes when I'm sitting around talking to people. I don't even have to peel them; I just pop them into my mouth. They're almost like little pieces of candy. And I know that grapes are really good for me; they have lots of iron in them. Grapes are sort of a favorite of mine too. How many of you like grapes? *(Pause for response.)*

Here's a beautiful apple. *(Hold up an apple.)* How many of you like apples? *(Pause for response.)* Apples are good for me too. And if they're crunchy and juicy, I really like them.

But I have a little confession to make. I'm not crazy about apples. They are not my favorite fruit. I know that they're good; I simply don't care for them that much. In fact this apple will probably be the last thing that I eat out of the fruit basket.

Unless I let this pear go too. *(Hold up a pear.)* A friend of mine says that pears are his favorite fruit. How many of you like pears? *(Pause for response.)* Great! I'm glad that some people do, because I simply don't care for them that much. I don't have a special reason; I know that pears are good fruits. I just don't care for them.

I'm sure that some of the fruits in this basket will disappear right away, because they are my favorites. Others will stay in the basket until there's nothing else left, because I don't care for them very much.

I think we're all like that, aren't we? We all have favorites—favorite fruits, favorite candies, favorite colors, even favorite people.

[*Note:* If you have time and want to have more involvement, you can extend the lesson here by asking about favorites: "Whose favorite color is red?" "Whose favorite fruit is oranges?"—raising your hand as you ask each question to encourage a like response.]

There's one Person who has absolutely no favorites, especially when it comes to people. Does anyone know who that is? I can give you a hint. He loves us all equally. We are all his favorites. *(Pause for response.)* That's right, it's God. The Bible tells us that we are all equal in God's sight.

If we were like these little fruits all piled up in a basket in front of God *(indicate the fruit basket)*, he wouldn't pick us over, would he? *(Shake your head to elicit the proper response.)* He wouldn't say, "Here's Susie, I like her best." *(Pull one fruit out of the basket.)* Or, "Here's Mark, he's one of my favorites." *(Pull another fruit out of the basket.)* And then look at the rest of us *(indicate the remaining fruits in the basket)* and say, "They're okay, but I don't really like them that much." *(Put the fruits back in the basket.)*

No! God looks at us all through Jesus *(indicate the complete fruit basket)* and says, "They're all my children, and I love them all very much." You are all God's children, and he loves each one of you, no matter how different you are from one another.

So the next time you pick out a favorite—maybe a

favorite fruit *(indicate the basket)* or a favorite color, or a favorite candy, that's okay. People always have favorites. But, when you think of a favorite, you can remember that God doesn't have favorites. He loves each one of us.

33

Plant a Tree

Scripture: He is like a tree planted by streams of water, which yields its fruit in season and whose leaf does not wither. Whatever he does prospers (Ps. 1:3).

Concept: God will bless those who are rooted in him.

Object: A tree seedling or sapling

I wanted to show you what I've been doing this week, so I saved a sample and brought it along. *(Show them the seedling.)* I've been planting trees!

I know that this doesn't look much like a tree yet. It's small; it's got a long way to go before it's a good, strong tree. But, if I plant it right, it should do well.

How can I plant this well? What should I do to make sure that it grows? *(Pause for response.)* That's right; I should make sure that I get the roots *(show them the roots)* down firmly in soil. I'll even pack the soil around it a bit when I plant it. And I should be sure that it gets enough water. I can't plant it near a river or stream, so I'll have to be very faithful about watering it if there's not much rain this spring.

I expect this tree to grow well if I plant it well. Eventually it should be straight and tall, taller than any of us. And, when it's big enough it will make pine cones. *(Name the fruit of that seedling.)* Plant a tree well, and it will grow well.

The Bible says that the same thing is true about us. In fact the Bible compares us to trees. It says that people who delight in God's Word are like trees planted by streams of water. They grow strong and have a lot of fruit. That means they grow up to be good, strong Christians.

Just like this tree *(show them the seedling)* needs good soil to grow well, so you need good advice—good *do's* and *don'ts*—to grow the way God wants you to grow. The best soil for you, the best rules for living, are found in God's Word, the Bible. And, just like this tree needs water to refresh it, so you need someone who loves you and will help you. God loves you very much and has promised to help you.

Is there someone who would like to plant this tree for me? *(Pause for response and pick a volunteer.)* Make sure that you plant it well so that it will grow well.

Only one person here can plant that tree for me. But all of you can plant "trees" that are much more important—yourselves! Just make sure that you're planted well, that you listen to the Bible—God's Word to you—and you live the way God wants you to live. Then God will bless you and help you grow into a strong Christian.

34

Happy Day!

Scripture: This is the day the LORD has made; let us rejoice and be glad in it (Ps. 118:24).

Concept: Every day is a good day in the Lord.

Object: This is best done on a dreary, rainy day. Have the children sit where they can look out of a window. If the day isn't dreary or the children can't see outside, take a picture of a dark cloud with rain falling from it.

Good morning! (*Say it with a bright, cheery smile.*) It's a great day, isn't it?

I have a feeling that some of you don't agree with me. Don't you think it's a great day? (*Shake your head as you ask the question to elicit a similar response.*)

I know what's wrong. (*Point to the window.*) It's dark and rainy. We can't go out to play; we probably won't see the sun all day. It looks like it might rain the whole day. Sometimes this gloomy weather can make us feel gloomy too.

(*Or [alternate object]*) I have a picture of a cloud, a certain type of cloud. Can anyone tell me what kind of cloud it is? (*Pause for response.*) That's right, it's a rain cloud! You can tell because there's rain coming down from it.

Let's pretend that you saw rain clouds when you came to church this morning. It was dark and dreary, and it looked like it might rain the whole day.

How would you feel—maybe a little gloomy? You'd know that you couldn't go out to play. Maybe you wouldn't see the sun all day. Sometimes gloomy weather can make us feel gloomy too.

There's no reason to feel gloomy; it's still a great day! We need rain to make the plants grow. We need rain clouds to bring the rain. On a gloomy day like this, we can just remind ourselves that God is watering the earth. Then we can be happy and thank him for the rain.

Every day is a great day, no matter what the weather may be. Do you know why? Because every day comes from God! The Bible says: "This is the day the LORD has made; let us rejoice and be glad in it."

So let's be happy! Be happy that God sent the rain. Be happy that God gave us this day to enjoy. Be happy that God gave us life and each other to enjoy. Be happy that God gave us so many blessings to enjoy. And be happy that God loves us and wants us to enjoy this day.

No matter what the weather, we don't have to feel gloomy. God is in control of everything. He loves us, and he's given us another good day. This is the day that the Lord has made. Rejoice, and be glad!

35

A Place for You

Scripture: It was he who gave some to be apostles, some to be prophets, some to be evangelists, and some to be pastors and teachers (Eph. 4:11).

Concept: Each of us has been given what he or she needs to fill his or her place in God's kingdom.

Objects: A spider in a jar, a housefly in another jar, a bee in another jar, a worm in another jar (*Note:* Use as many of these as time will allow. Provisions are made for all of them.)

I brought several of God's little creatures with me today, because I want to talk about their place in creation. Maybe you already know some of those places.

(Show them the spider.) What is a spider's place in creation? Can you tell me why God made spiders? *(Pause for response.)* That's right, spiders help keep insects in check. If we didn't have spiders, we would have far too many bugs in the world. God made spiders to help keep the bug population in check.

That's why God gave spiders tiny little silk-making glands. Every spider that you see can make silk, so that it can wrap up the bugs it catches or can make a web to catch bugs with. God gave spiders just what they need to catch bugs.

(Show them the housefly.) Does anyone know a housefly's place in creation? Let me help you with that one. Where do you usually see flies? *(Pause for response.)* Right, you usually see them on garbage or in other icky places. That's a housefly's place in creation. It helps clean up garbage.

God made houseflies so that they don't get sick from all those germs. We would if we ate the things they eat. But they don't because God made them that way so they could clean up the garbage. And he gave them special mouths, just right for cleaning up the garbage that we don't want to touch.

(Show them the bee.) Does anyone know a bee's place in creation? *(Pause for response.)* That's right, a bee makes honey that's good for us to eat. And as a bee flies from flower to flower it helps those flowers make seeds.

That's why God made a bee so hairy. Pollen, that yellow dust from flowers, sticks to the hairy bee and is spread easily from flower to flower. God even gave the bee a special wax-making "machine" inside its body, so that it can make honeycomb to store the honey in.

(Show them the worm.) How about worms? Does anyone know a worm's place in creation? *(Pause for response.)* That's right, a worm helps give us good dirt. If God didn't put worms in the ground for us, we probably wouldn't be able to grow the foods that we grow. Worms help give us rich dirt.

God gave this worm very special insides, so that it

can eat dirt. And, somehow, the worm helps make the dirt rich and good for growing plants.

Each of these little creatures has a special place in creation. In fact, all of God's creatures do. And God gave each creature exactly what it needs to fill its place.

What about us? We're God's special creatures. The Bible tells us that we are much more important to God than any of these little creatures. Does each of us have a special place in God's kingdom? *(Pause for response.)* Of course we do! And God gives each one of us exactly what we need to fill our place in his kingdom.

You may not know what you're going to be when you grow up. But you can know that God gave you talents to do something special.

And you don't have to wait until you're grown up. Each of you has a place in God's kingdom right now. And each of you has something special to fill that place.

Do you like to talk? You can tell others about Jesus. Maybe you're shy, but a very steady friend. You can be a friend to the lonely. Maybe you're generous, and can help needy people. Each one of you has a special talent that you can use for Jesus. And each one of you has a special place to use it.

The next time you see a spider [a fly, a bee, and/or a worm] you can think of the special place that it has in creation. And that can remind you that God has a special place for you, and he has given you very special talents to fill that place.

36

God Cares for You

Scripture: "If that is how God clothes the grass of the field, which is here today, and tomorrow is thrown into the fire, how much more will he clothe you, O you of little faith!" (Luke 12:28).

Concept: God will take care of you.

Objects: A few clumps of grass, roots and all. Take at least one clump out a week in advance, so it will turn brown. It would be good to get at least one clump with a few grass flowers (those brushy-looking things) on top.

Who can tell me what this is? *(Show the children the clumps of grass and pause for response.)* That's right, it's grass. I dug this up, roots and all, because I want to show you some neat things about grass. We walk over grass all the time, but we really don't know very much about it.

First, look at these roots. *(Show the children the roots.)* They're very thick. Not all plants have such thick, tangled roots but grass does. Those roots help the grass stay in the ground, right where it belongs. They also help hold dirt in the ground so that it won't blow away. Sometimes I think that God gave grass such thick, tangled roots because he knew we would be walking all over it, so he helps it stay in place and helps dirt stay in place.

Can you see the stems on some of the grass? *(Try to point out some grass stems.)* God made these stems special too. He made them so that they can grow well even after they're cut. Not all stems grow like that. If you cut all the flower stems in your garden, the flowers probably wouldn't grow back. But when you cut grass stems, you help them grow. Sometimes I think that God made grass stems like that because he knew that we would be cutting grass so much. He made it very sturdy and able to grow back easily.

Did you know that God made even little grass flowers? *(If you have some grass flowers, point them out to the children.)* They don't look like much. They're not big and showy, you can't smell them, and you'd never pick them for a pretty bouquet. But God made them perfect for grass. They're short, so they don't always get cut. Nobody picks them, because they're not that pretty. So all the little flowers grow to make lots of grass seeds. And the seeds can spill out onto the grass to make even more grass.

Did you know that lots of animals eat grass? They do, and it's good for them. Maybe that's why God made so much grass and made it so hardy, able to grow quite easily.

When I look at grass, I think that God really takes good care of it. He knew how much we were going to use it and how important it was going to be. So he gave it special roots and special stems and special flowers. Did you know that Jesus talked about grass?

He said that God takes good care of his grass. We found that out just by looking at it.

But Jesus went on to say that God will take even better care of us. We are much more important to God than all the grass in the world. We are his special creatures, and he loves us very much. God knows what we need even before we ask him for it. And he will give us what we need, just like he gave the grass what it needs. Only he will give us much, much more and take very good care of us. Jesus has promised that, because he loves us so much.

So when you walk over your lawn, or help someone mow the grass, or even walk down a sidewalk and look at grass, that can remind you of God's care. You can think of the neat roots and stems and leaves that God gave grass. And then you can remember that God will give you everything you need. He's promised always to care for you because he loves you very much.

37

He Loves Me, He Loves Me, He Loves Me!

Scripture: God is love. Whoever lives in love lives in God, and God in him (1 John 4:16).

Concept: God loves us!

Object: A daisy

There's a little game we used to play with daisies like this. *(Show them the daisy and begin to pull off a few petals as you speak.)* He loves me, he loves me not, he loves me, he loves me not. The last petal would tell whether he loves me or not. If it came off with "He loves me," that would mean that the person I'm thinking about loved me. If the last petal came off as I said, "He loves me not," that would mean that the person didn't love me.

How many of you have done that with daisies? *(Pause for response.)* You think of a certain person and then you say, "he [or she] loves me, he loves me not," as you take off the petals, right down to the last petal.

That doesn't really work, does it? A flower can't tell you if a person loves you or not. We know that's just a little game.

But we also know that some people love us and some people don't. Some people don't even know us. How can they love us if they don't know us? And some people don't love us even if they do know us. It's too bad, but that's just the way people are. Although we should, we don't love everybody we know. And everybody we know doesn't love us.

But there is one Person who always loves you. He always has and he always will. No matter what you do, he will always love you. Do you know who that is? *(Pause for response.)*

That's right, it's God [or Jesus]! God tells us in the Bible that he loves us. He loves us so much that he sent Jesus to die for our sins. [Or, Jesus loves us so much that he died for us.]

Before you were born, God knew who you were. And he loved you then already. Right now he loves you, and he wants you to love him, too. No matter what happens, he will always love you.

Isn't that great? God loves you. He wants only what's best for you, and he has promised always to love you. He watches over you in love all the time. And all he wants is for you to love him too.

So the next time you see a daisy, you can play the little game. But you can be absolutely sure that the game is going to work. Think of God as you pull off the petals and then say, "He loves me, he loves me, he loves me." *(Pull off a few more petals as you speak.)* And it will come out right every time. Because God surely does love you!

38

Working Together

Scripture: Now to each one the manifestation of the Spirit is given for the common good (1 Cor. 12:7).

Concept: God has given each of us a job to do for his kingdom.

Object: An ant in a jar

I caught an ant out on the sidewalk yesterday, put it in a jar, and took it along to show you this morning. *(Hold up the jar so that they can see the ant.)* But I'm going to be sure to put this ant back exactly where I found it after we're finished talking about it this morning.

Do you know why I'm going to return this ant? Because I know that it has a job to do, and that other ants were depending on it.

Although this ant was wandering alone, I know that it belongs to a big ant city. Somewhere near where I found it, there are lots of other ants all living and working together. This ant is a part of that group.

It was probably out wandering in search of food for the ant city. Most of the ants that you see are out looking for food for their cities. That's their job.

Back in the ant city, other ants are working to keep their place clean. Some are taking care of the ant eggs, or the tiny ants that hatch from them. Other ants are probably helping to enlarge the ant city. And still other ants are doing different jobs around their ant city.

Each ant was created to do a certain job in its ant city. So each ant does the job that it can do and depends on other ants to do other jobs for it. They all work together to keep the ant city running well.

That's just the way that God created ants: each able to do different jobs, and all to work together for their common good.

That's the way God made us, too. He gave each of us different talents and abilities.

[*Note:* If you know the children well, mention some of them by name with some outstanding characteristic. If not, general suggestions are given below.]

Somebody may be very good working with his or her hands, able to fix almost anything. Someone else maybe can't do that at all but is a whiz at math or another school subject. Someone else maybe is the most patient person you know, good at working with other people. And maybe you're extra friendly, good at talking to people. Each one of us has some talent that God has given us, something that we are particularly good at.

God wants each one of us to use our talent for the good of all his people. He said in the Bible that each of these talents is given for our common good. In other words, use the talent you have to help God's people. If you're good at working with your hands, help people build and fix things. If you're a whiz at some subject, study that and share what you know. If you're good at working with people or talking to them, be sure that you share the Good News of Jesus with them. That's for their good. All of our talents should be used to help others so that we can all work together.

So after the service, I'm going to put this ant back. Then it can do its job. And when you see ants walking along the sidewalk, they can help you remember: Just like them, God created us each with different talents to do different things. And he wants us to work together for our common good.

39

Those Bible *Nots*

Scripture: Submit yourselves, then, to God.
Resist the devil, and he will flee from you
(James 4:7).

Concept: God tells us not to do certain things
because he loves us.

Object: A live bumblebee, a honeybee, or a
wasp in a jar (*Note:* Any stinging, yellow and
black "buzzer" will work.)

Look what I caught this week! (*Show them the jar.*) I had quite a time catching this. Some insects are easy to catch. You simply pick them up and put them in a jar. But not a bumblebee [or whatever you have in the jar]. I had to wait until this bee sat on a flower and then quickly clamp the jar over it. I didn't want to catch it with my bare hands.

Would any of you catch a bee with your bare hands? (*Pause for response.*) Of course not! It might sting you.

Generally we avoid any insect that's colored yellow and black and goes "Buzzz" when it flies. We know that yellow and black insects that buzz usually have stingers, so we stay away from them. Their colors and their buzzing are a good warning sign, and we pay attention to the warning.

I think that God had us in mind when he gave bees their color and their buzz. He didn't want us hurt, so he gave us a very clear warning: "Here's something that may hurt you; stay away from it."

God gave us other clear warnings of things that might harm us. It's good for us to know the warning signs, so that we can stay away from those things. One of the most important warning signs in the Bible is the word *not*.

Can anyone think of something God told us not to do? *(Pause for response. If responses are not forthcoming, help them out with the rest of this paragraph.)* Maybe I can help you out. Think of the Ten Commandments; aren't there some *nots* in there? How about "Thou shalt not steal"? Or "Thou shalt not murder"? Didn't God tell us not to worship anything except him? Didn't he tell us not to use his name in vain?

That sounds like a lot of *nots*, doesn't it? It almost sounds like God doesn't want us to do anything.

But that's not the case at all. Those *nots* that you hear in the Bible are God's warnings to us. He loves us and wants only what is best for us. He wants us to stay out of trouble, so there are some things he tells us not to do. Those *nots* are clear warnings for our own good.

Those *nots* in the Bible are, in a way, like this bee. When we see its colors and hear it buzz, we know immediately that we shouldn't catch it with our bare hands. We stay away from it to avoid harm. And when we hear from the Bible things that we should *not* do, we know immediately that we should pay attention. God is giving us a clear warning, because he loves us and wants to keep us from harm.

40

No Weeds in Christ

Scripture: You are all one in Christ Jesus (Gal. 3:28).

Concept: Everyone is equal in God's sight through Jesus Christ.

Object: A bouquet of flowers. Be sure to include at least one kind of "weed" (dandelion, goldenrod, chickweed, chickory, and so forth) and a few garden flowers.

(*Note:* Exactly what you say about each flower depends on the flowers you have chosen. A few examples are given below. Begin with the garden flowers on one side of the bouquet and the so-called weeds on the other.)

I've brought a bouquet of flowers with me today. Aren't they pretty? Let's see if we can name some of them.

Who can tell me what this flower is? (*Pull one "garden" flower from the bouquet and pause for response.*) That's right, it's a rose. It certainly is beautiful, isn't it? And it smells so nice. Lots of people love to have roses blooming near their houses. They often spend a lot of time trying to make roses grow. Does anyone here have roses growing near their house?

What is this flower? *(Pull another garden flower from the bouquet and pause for response.)* It's a daisy! People love daisies, too. Daisies often grow in gardens. They may not smell as nice as roses do, but they certainly are cheerful flowers.

Does anyone know what this flower is? *(Pull one more garden flower from the bouquet and pause for response.)* It's a sunflower. I love to grow sunflowers. They're always so big and bright. And they bring birds to my garden. Birds like to eat the seeds of sunflowers. Sunflowers are great plants to have in a flower garden.

Here's another flower. What is this one? *(Pull out a "weed" and pause for response.)* That's right; it's a dandelion! Everyone knows this one. I think it's a really cheerful flower. It can grow almost anyplace and add a touch of color to any lawn.

Not everyone likes this flower, do they? *(Shake your head to elicit the proper response.)* Some people hate to have dandelions growing in their lawns. They work hard to keep dandelions away. They call dandelions "weeds."

This is another one that people don't often like. *(Show them another weed.)* It's called "goldenrod." I think it's a beautiful flower, but lots of people call it a weed. You can see goldenrod growing alongside the highways, but you don't often see it in gardens. For some strange reason, people don't like goldenrod, so they call it a weed, just like the dandelion.

Some people call these *(indicate the garden flowers)* flowers and these *(indicate the weeds)* weeds. Yet I can't see any difference between them, can you? *(Pause for response.)* They all look like pretty flowers to me.

We can use these flowers to remind us of the way God looks at us. When God looks down at his children, he doesn't see some flowers and some weeds. God doesn't say, "There's David, one of my flowers. I really love him." *(Indicate a garden flower.)* And there's Susie. I love her, but not quite as much." *(Indicate a weed.)* God doesn't divide us into flowers and weeds. We're all precious flowers to him. *(Indicate the whole bouquet.)*

The Bible tells us that, as long as we believe in Jesus, we are all equal in God's sight. We are all his children, his special flowers, and he loves each one of us very much.

41

We Belong to God

Scripture: Know that the LORD is God. It is he who made us, and we are his (Ps. 100:3).

Concept: God made us, and we belong to him.

Objects: Some small creature (such as a spider, an ant, a worm) in a glass jar; a picture (which you drew) of that creature; a picture of the children (you can draw one, or paste one together from a pictorial directory). (*Note:* You can expand the lesson by adding more pictures of living creatures and the creatures themselves.)

I took a picture along to show you. (*Show them the picture.*) It's a picture of a _____. You may not think this picture is very good, but I'm proud of it. You see, I made it myself. I drew this picture and I colored it. It took me a long time to make this picture. I wanted it to look like a real _____, so I put a lot of work into it; I'm rather proud of it.

Tell me, who owns this picture? Whom does this picture belong to? (*Point to yourself as you ask the questions, so that they can't miss the point. Pause for response.*)

Right, it's mine. I'm not about to give it away. I like it and I'm going to keep it. I made it and it's mine.

I have the real thing with me, too. *(Show them the creature.)* I picked this up yesterday, just so that you could see it.

Of course, the real _____ is a lot better than the picture. This _____ is alive and walking all over the jar. Could I make this _____? I couldn't possibly make a real, living _____.

Who made this real _____? *(Pause for response.)* Of course, God did. Only God can make real, living creatures.

If God made this _____, then to whom does it belong? *(Pause for response.)* Yes, it belongs to God. God made it, and it's his. I just borrowed it for a little while so that I could show it to you. I have it in the jar right now, but it's really God's _____.

[*Note:* You can expand this lesson at this point. If you have other pictures and little creatures, repeat the above paragraphs using them. You may want to shorten each paragraph a little, so that the point (I made it, it's mine; God made it, it's his) becomes more and more obvious.]

Now I've got one more picture to show you. *(Show them the picture of children.)* Can you tell what this is? *(Pause for response.)* Yes, it's a picture of children. I made this picture, too. This is really a picture of you! Here's Susie, here's Mark, here's Sara, [and so forth]. *(Name real children in your audience and point to individual children in the picture as you speak.)*

This is my picture. I made it and it belongs to me. I'm going to keep it to remind me of you all week long.

But do you belong to me? Of course not!

Who made you? To whom do you belong? *(Pause for response.)* Of course, God made you! Just like God made all living creatures, he also made you. And, just like this _____ [and this _____, and this _____] belong to him, you also belong to him.

The Bible tells us that, just so that we won't forget. It says: "Know that the LORD is God. It is he who made us, and we are his."

We didn't make ourselves. God made us, and we belong to him.

You know that God made you his very special creature, don't you? He made you much better than this _____ [and this _____ and this _____]. He made you in his image, able to love him and to know that you belong to him.

This _____ doesn't know it belongs to God. [Neither does this _____ and this _____.] But you do. Every time you see a _____ [and a _____ and a _____] you can think, "God made that little living creature. It belongs to him." And that can remind you that God made you, too. He made you his special creature. He loves you very much, and you belong to him.

42

Be Still and Know

Scripture: "Be still, and know that I am God."
(Ps. 46:10).

Concept: At times we should sit quietly to listen
to God.

Object: A cocoon (If you can't find one, use a
picture.)

Who can tell me what this is? *(Hold up the
cocoon and pause for response.)* That's right, it's a cocoon.
I found it just this week, so I carefully cut it out of the
bush it was in and took it to show to you.

Who knows what kind of little creature makes a
cocoon? *(Pause for response.)* Yes, a caterpillar. Some
time in the last few weeks, a little caterpillar crawled
near my bushes. It went right up one of the branches
and spun itself this cocoon.

Some time next spring this cocoon will break open
and what will fly out? *(Pause for response.)* Yes, a beautiful moth!

[*Note:* Generally moths come from cocoons and butterflies come from chrysalids. *Moth* is used here for accuracy, although you may feel more comfortable with "butterfly."]

It won't be at all like the caterpillar that spun this cocoon. It will be a beautiful moth.

Right now, that little caterpillar is resting inside this cocoon, becoming a beautiful moth. It's resting quietly. Can you see this cocoon move at all? *(Hold the cocoon up steadily.)* No! This cocoon is perfectly quiet.

It has to rest; it has to have a quiet time before it can become a moth. That's the way God made it. If that little caterpillar didn't spin a cocoon to rest in, it probably would never become a moth. If it kept crawling around, eating leaves and didn't take time to rest, it would just stay a caterpillar. So God made it to have a quiet time. While it's resting quietly inside this cocoon, God changes it from a caterpillar into a moth.

In a way we're sort of like the little caterpillar inside of this cocoon. Doesn't that sound strange? But it isn't. Just like God made this little caterpillar to have a quiet time, God also made us to have quiet times.

In the Bible God says to us, "Be still, and know that I am God." Sometimes he just wants us to sit quietly and listen to him.

How can we listen to God? *(Pause for response.)* That's right, we can sit quietly and listen when the Bible is read. We can sit quietly and listen when people talk about the Bible, or when the minister preaches from the Bible. And we sit quietly when we talk to God—when we pray.

It's not always easy to sit quietly, is it? Sometimes we just want to keep on doing whatever we're doing. We like to run and jump and play. And that's good too.

But we can't run and jump and play forever. God wants us to have quiet time, too. That's why he said, "Be still and know that I am God."

Just like the little caterpillar inside this cocoon, God made us to need quiet times, although we don't always feel like having them. But if we are quiet and listen to God, he will use that time to make us into beautiful Christians. Just like he's using this caterpillar's quiet time to make it into a beautiful moth.

43

God's Word Forever

Scripture: "The grass withers and the flowers fall, but the word of our God stands forever" (Isa. 40:8).

Concept: God's Word stands forever.

Objects: A (wild) flower that's beginning to die; some leaves that have changed color, and a Bible

(*Note:* This object lesson works best during autumn.)

I brought a flower with me today, but it looks like it's seen better days. (*Show them the flower.*) I think that it's dying. It's not dying just because I picked it. It looked like this when I found it. I think it was ready to die.

Most flowers don't last that long, not even when they're growing on healthy plants. They're beautiful for a little while, but then they shrivel up and die.

These leaves (*show them the leaves*) lasted a bit longer, I think. They probably were green and healthy all summer. But they're done now too. They changed color and fell off the tree. I picked these up off the ground. They're dead.

That's just the way it is with all plants. They don't live forever. They grow green and healthy for a while, but finally they grow old and die. We can see that especially this time of the year. Leaves are falling off the trees; plants are withering and dying.

But then, all things grow old and fall apart or die. The trees that these leaves came from will finally die and fall over. The plants that these flowers were on will wither and die. Anything that you see outside will finally grow old and die. Can you name any growing thing that will not die? *(Pause for response. If the children volunteer some answers, show how each thing they name will eventually fall apart or die.)*

Even the things that you see in this church will finally wear out. The windows may break, the carpet will wear out. Some day we may have to put in new furniture. Even the building will grow old and creaky. Nothing lasts forever.

Wait a minute. Am I correct when I say that *nothing* lasts forever? *(Shake your head as you ask the question to encourage the same response.)* No! There is something that will last forever. Can anyone tell me what that is? Let me give you a hint. *(Show them the Bible and pause for response.)* That's right, the Bible.

We know that this book won't last forever. It will wear out. But the Bible tells us that God's Word will stand forever. What God tells us in this Book will never grow old. It will never die, it will never be out of date, it will always stand. We can always count on God's Word to us; we can always count on his promises and his love.

128

Who can tell me some of God's promises? *(Pause for response and discuss each promise as it is mentioned.)* Let me help you. Did God promise that he would always love us? Did God promise that he would never leave us? Did God promise to forgive our sins through Jesus? *(Wait for response.)*

All of those promises are in the Bible, God's Word to us. And God told us that his Word will stand forever. Those promises to us are good forever and ever. We can always count on God to keep his promises—his Word—to us.

44

God's Constant Love (Valentine's Day)

Scripture: For I am convinced that neither death nor life . . . neither the present nor the future . . . nor anything else in all creation, will be able to separate us from the love of God that is in Christ Jesus our Lord (Rom. 8:38, 39).

Concept: God will always love us.

Objects: Four or five valentines

Does anyone know what day is coming up this week? I'll give you a hint; some people send out valentines for that day. *(Pause for response.)* Right, Wednesday [or whatever day] will be Valentine's Day. Some people send out hearts to other people, just to say "I love you," or "I'm thinking of you."

I usually don't send valentines, but I decided to send a few this year. So I brought them along to show you before I send them. *(Show them the valentines, then place them at your side.)*

Some of these are special, for people who are special

to me. *(Pick up the valentines one by one as you talk about them. Put them on a separate stack when you are finished with them.)* This is for my husband [or wife, or a very special friend]. I'm sure that he knows I love him, but I thought it would be nice to send a valentine for a change. This one is special, too. _____ is a special friend of mine, and I thought he/she would enjoy getting this in the mail.

This one is a little different. It's for _____.
_____ isn't really a close friend of mine, but I think of him/her every once in a while. I thought that it was time to get in touch again, so a valentine will be a nice way to do it. Someone else I don't think about very often is _____. I like him; we just don't stay in touch. So I thought I'd send him a valentine, too.

[*Note:* Continue in this manner (people I don't think of often, or don't know very well, but want to send a valentine to) until all the valentines have been used.]

I expect that I may receive a few valentines, too. Probably about as many as I send. *(Pick up the stack again and riffle through them.)* One or two may be from [your spouse and/or very special friends]. And then some will be from people I don't think about very often, like _____ and _____ [the people you named previously].

Do you know what's going to happen to all of these valentines? I'll look at them for a while, and remember those people. But finally I'll have to throw the valentines away or recycle them. I just don't have room to keep them. If you get valentines, are you going to keep them forever? Probably not. We'll probably all get rid of them after a week or two.

The sad thing is, I'll probably forget about those

people again, too. Oh, not [your spouse and/or very special friends], but _____ and _____ , those people I don't keep in touch with. I'll probably forget about them for several days or weeks, until they call or write, or something like that. I'll look at their valentines *(pick up a valentine)*, say, "Oh, that's nice," and then throw it away *(indicate throwing the valentine in a waste/recycle basket)* and forget about them. They'll probably do the same with my valentines and they'll probably forget about me, too.

That's the way people are. Not everybody; not your parents! But other people sometimes send you valentines, and are really friendly. And then they forget about you after a while. Even friends do that sometimes, don't they? They can be your best friends one day, and then the next day it seems like they change their minds.

There's one Person who will never change his mind and will never forget you. He loves you very much now, and he will always love you very much. Who do you think that is? *(Pause for response.)* That's right, it's God!

The Bible says that God loves you now, God loves you all the time, and God will always love you. He doesn't need a valentine to remember you. He's with you all the time; he won't forget you. And he won't stop loving you.

So when you decide to put away any valentines you may get, look them over one more time. Try to remember the people that give them to you. But especially remember, as you put them away, that God will never "put you away." He will always remember you, and he will always love you.

45

Easter

Scripture: But Christ has indeed been raised from the dead, the firstfruits of those who have fallen asleep. . . . For as in Adam all die, so in Christ all will be made alive (1 Cor. 15:20, 22).

Concept: Jesus rose from the dead to give us eternal life.

Objects: A few brightly colored Easter eggs

All of you know what these are, right? *(Show them the eggs.)* They're Easter eggs! I brought a few of mine along from home.

How many of you have Easter eggs at home? *(Pause for response.)* Lots of people have Easter eggs this time of the year; even some people who don't know what Easter really is. They just think that colored eggs are pretty to have around, so they decorate with Easter eggs.

But for us Easter eggs can be really special because they can remind us of the meaning of Easter.

Think about eggs for a minute. What hatches from

an egg? *(Pause for response.)* That's right, a brand-new baby bird! Before the bird hatches, the egg just sits there; it doesn't look alive at all. *(As you speak, cup your hands into an egg shape, still at first, and then hatching open.)* But then it shakes a little and breaks open, and out comes a brand-new life! It's the wonder of creation, the way an egg can produce a brand-new life!

So we often use eggs to remind us of new life. We look at an egg and say, "God can bring life out of that egg." An egg can remind us of new life.

Now, let's think about Easter for a minute. Who can tell me what wonderful thing happened on the very first Easter? *(Pause for response.)* That's right, Jesus rose from the dead! He had been dead and buried, and he rose from the dead. He walked out of this tomb! He showed us that God is more powerful than death!

Now Jesus promises us that we can live forever with him in heaven. We will never die in heaven; we will always live with him. We believe Jesus' promise, because we know that he is more powerful than death. We know that Jesus can give us life forever because he rose from the dead on that first Easter.

Easter is all about new life, isn't it? On Easter we celebrate the time that Jesus rose from the dead. And because of Easter, we know that we can live forever with Jesus.

So, these Easter eggs can remind us of very special things. We see an egg, and we think of new life. And then we remember that Jesus rose from the dead so that we could live forever with him in heaven.

46

The Earth Is the Lord's (Earth Day)

Scripture: The earth is the LORD's, and everything in it, the world, and all who live in it (Ps. 24:1).

Concept: Because everything in the world belongs to God, we should be careful how we use it.

Objects: Pictures of creatures and plants—enough so that each child can have one

I brought enough pictures with me today so that each of you can hold one for a little while. *(Pass out the pictures and continue to speak as you do so.)* I spent a lot of time finding just the right pictures and cutting them out. Please be careful with them. They're still my pictures; I'm just lending them to you for a little while. I may ask to have them back, so be very careful with them. Meanwhile you may hold them. You may look at them and think about the little creatures you see pictured on them, but don't wrinkle them or ruin them because I may ask to have them back. Treat them carefully.

Let's talk about these pictures for a little while. Who can tell me what their picture shows? *(Pause for response. Exactly how you proceed depends on which pictures you have chosen. Examples are given below.)*

A bird! Can you hold the picture up so that everyone can see it? Isn't that pretty? And that's only a picture. I love real birds, don't you? They sing so nicely and add such a beautiful touch of life to our backyards. I picked out that picture to remind me of how pretty real birds are.

Who made all the pretty birds? *(Pause for response.)* That's right, God did! We can't make birds, can we? No! We can make pictures of them, but only God can make real birds. He made all the birds. They all belong to him.

Put that picture down very carefully, please. *(Address this to the child holding the picture of the bird.)* I want to keep that picture.

Who else can tell me what their picture shows? *(Call on one child for a response.)*

A fish! Hold the picture up carefully so that everyone can see it. Some people think that fish aren't very pretty, but I think that they're neat. Just think, they can swim underwater forever, and they don't drown! They don't have any arms and legs, and yet they move about with no problem. And they can live in water that's much colder than we could ever swim in. I don't see fish very often, so I picked out this picture to remind me of how neat fish really are.

Who made the fish so neat? *(Pause for response.)* That's right, God did! We can't make fish, can we? No! We can make pictures of them, but only God can make real, living fish. God made all the fish in the world; they all belong to him.

Put that picture down very carefully, please. *(Address this to the child holding the picture of the fish.)* I want to keep that picture to remind me of all the neat fish God made.

(Proceed in this manner. Ask a child to hold up a picture and mention some facts about the creature or plant pictured. Ask the children who made that creature and say that God made it so it belongs to him. Finish each section by asking the child to put the picture down very carefully because it's yours and you want to keep it.)

Have you noticed how I asked you to treat these pictures? Every time we were finished with one, I asked you to put it down "very carefully." That's because they're my pictures, and I want to keep them looking nice. So I asked you to treat them with care.

But those are only pictures. What about the creatures and plants we mentioned? Whom do they belong to? *(Pause for response.)* That's right! We said over and over that God made those creatures; they belong to him. God made the living birds, the neat fish, and so on, and they all belong to him. The pictures may be mine, but the real creatures are God's.

How do you think God wants us to treat his creations? *(Pause for response.)* That's right! He wants us to be careful with them. After all, he made them and he gave them life. We can look at them and see how neat they are. I think he put them in the world for us to enjoy. He's "lending" them to us for a little while, but they still belong to him. So we should be very careful with all of these things, because they belong to God.

Now, I changed my mind about the pictures. I'm giving them to you. You may take them home and do what you want with them. I would be happy if you would hang them up for a while. Then you can look at them and think about God's creations. The picture is now yours, but the real, living plants and creatures belong to God. Enjoy God's creations, but please, be very careful with them.

47

The Language of Prayer (Prayer Day)

Scripture: The LORD . . . hears the prayer of the righteous (Prov. 15:29).

Concept: God hears the sincere prayer, no matter how it is uttered.

Object: A jar of ants

I brought a jar of ants with me today because I want to talk to you about prayer. When I see ants, I often think about how God hears my prayers. You may think that's strange, but if you listen closely I think you'll understand what I mean.

Did you know that ants talk to each other? They really do. They speak a language that we can't understand. In fact we can't even hear them talk.

Have you ever heard an ant speak? *(Pause for response.)* Of course not! No one has heard an ant speak because ants don't talk aloud. But they do speak to each other.

Watch these ants. *(Hold up the jar.)* If you can't see

them just close your eyes and imagine that you're watching ants scurry down a sidewalk. What do ants do when they meet each other? They stop and rub each other's feelers. Have you seen ants stop, put their heads together, and then go their separate ways?

Well, when ants do that, they're speaking to each other. Honest, they are! Each ant lets out a little bit of chemical—like a little puff of perfume—and the other ant "smells" that with its antennae and receives a message through the chemical. It's just like talking; it's the ants' way of speaking to each other. They give each other several messages this way. Now we can't hear ants speak to each other because it's a silent language. But they understand each other, and that's what counts.

That's often the way prayer is. Sometimes we pray aloud, but often we pray silently. No other person can hear us; but God can, and he understands exactly what we're saying to him and what we need.

All we have to do is sit quietly, think about God, and talk to him in our heads. He will hear us, even though we don't talk aloud. He understands that silent language of prayer.

Sometimes we may get mixed up, and the words may not even come out right in our heads. But if we're truly praying to God in our heads, he still can understand what we're saying.

No one else can hear us when we pray like this. But God listens and can understand us, and that's what counts. Now maybe you can understand why I think about prayer when I see ants talking to each other. Ants are tiny creatures, but they can remind us of something big in our lives: God always hears us when we pray to him.

48

The Holy Spirit (Pentecost)

Scripture: "The wind blows wherever it pleases. You hear its sound, but you cannot tell where it comes from or where it is going. So it is with everyone born of the Spirit" (John 3:8).

Concept: The Holy Spirit cannot be seen but can be felt.

Object: A small scrap of paper

I have nothing for you to look at today, because I want to talk about something that you can't see. But you can see what it does and you can feel it. I want to talk about the wind.

Is it windy in here right now? *(Pause for response.)* No, it's hardly ever windy inside of church, is it? *(Note: If fans are running, you might want to mention them and how a few people can feel the breeze.)* The walls keep the wind out.

But we can make our own little breezes if we want to. Try this. *(Demonstrate as you speak.)* Put your hand a few inches away from your mouth. Now, make your own breeze. Blow on your hand.

Can you feel that little bit of wind? *(Pause for response.)* Can you see it? *(Pause for response.)* That's the way wind is; you can feel it but you can't see it.

But you can see what the wind does. Watch closely to see what this wind is going to do. *(Put the scrap of paper in the palm of your hand, then blow it off.)*

What did that little bit of wind do? *(Pause for response.)* That's right, it blew the paper right off my hand and onto the floor.

Could you see the wind? *(Pause for response.)* No! But you could surely see what it did. That's the way the wind is; you can't see it but you can feel it and you can see what it does.

Now, this is only a tiny wind. *(Blow a few times to show the children that you mean the "wind" that you are making.)* Usually the wind is much stronger than the little bit we make when we blow.

Let's think for a minute about the real wind outside—the strong breezes that blow sometime. Close your eyes and pretend that you are outside on a windy day. You can hear the wind blow: *whooo, whooo, whooo* [wind sounds]. You can feel it. Hang onto your hat, the wind may blow it off! It's blowing your hair around right now. Look at the leaves and twigs blow along the sidewalk! Be careful, you don't want the wind to blow you right over!

You can open your eyes now. I know that was just pretend, but I hope it made you think about the wind. You can't see it. But you surely can feel it, and you can see what it does.

Jesus talked about the wind. He said just what we've been saying, that you can't see the wind, but you can feel it and you can see what it does. And then Jesus went on to say that the Holy Spirit is just like the wind. You can't see the Holy Spirit, but you can feel him and you can see what he does.

Can anyone tell me who the Holy Spirit is? *(Pause for response.)* That's right, the Holy Spirit is God. You can't see God, you can't see the Holy Spirit. But yet we know that the Holy Spirit is real, because we can see what he does.

When someone says that he or she believes in Jesus, we know that the Holy Spirit has been working in that person. The Holy Spirit persuaded that person to believe in Jesus. When people obey God and do what he wants them to do, we know that the Holy Spirit has been working to help those people obey God. When you say that you want to be a good Christian, you can know that the Holy Spirit is working in your heart to bring you close to God.

You can't see God working in your heart, but you can feel him work, can't you? He helps you want to be God's child.

The Holy Spirit is much more powerful than any wind. He can change people's lives; he can make them good Christians. You can't see him, but you can feel him work inside of you.

So the next time you go outside on a windy day, the wind can help you think of the Holy Spirit. When you feel that wind blowing against your face, you can think, "That's like the Holy Spirit." And you can ask the Holy Spirit to work in your heart to bring you close to him.

49

God's Beautiful Bouquet (Ethnic Diversity)

Scripture: "And with your blood you purchased men for God from every tribe and language and people and nation" (Rev. 5:9).

Concept: God's kingdom includes people of various colors and various cultural backgrounds.

Object: A bouquet of several different types of flowers

Look at the beautiful bouquet I picked [or bought] this week. I think a bouquet of different kinds of flowers is especially pretty. It's so varied and colorful.

It's true that each of these flowers is special in its own way. (*Point out various flowers as you talk about them. Suggestions are given below.*)

Dandelions are hardy and grow almost anywhere. Roses have a delicate perfume. Daisies add a touch of color to our meadows. Queen Anne's lace is really several tiny flowers growing together. Milkweed is several flowers together. Finches use fluff from the seeds in their nests. Vetch is colorful and good for the soil. Birds love sunflower seeds. Asters are hardy and bloom late into the fall. Goldenrod is also hardy and provides overnight shelter for many insects. Carnations always last long in a bouquet. Baby's breath is delicate but helps fill out a bouquet. Ferns add a touch of green, and help make the bouquet look softer.

Each of these flowers is pretty, but together they're even prettier. They give us a beautiful bouquet.

Sometimes I think that God looks at his people that way. God's people come from every race and nation on earth. Together they're like a beautiful bouquet of flowers.

We could think of ourselves as a bunch of tulips. We're somewhat different from each other, but we're all somewhat the same too. We all speak the same language, we all go to the same church, we all live rather near to each other. We're a bunch of God's beautiful tulips.

But God has other children very different from us, as different as a rose is from a tulip. Some of his children are brown, some are black, some are yellow, and some are white. Some come from far away China, some from Argentina, some from Borneo, and some from Africa. But they're all God's children because they love Jesus.

Sometimes when we live with a bunch of tulips we tend to forget that there are roses and daisies and dandelions blooming in other places. But they're out there, growing for Jesus just like we are. And together we all make a beautiful bouquet for God.

So, you tulips, you look beautiful to me just the way you are, and God loves you just the way you are. But if you ever meet roses or daisies or dandelions—Christians much different from you—you can remember that they, too, are a part of God's beautiful bouquet.

50

Abortion Protest

Scripture: "You shall not murder" (Exod. 20:13).

Concept: Abortion is killing unborn babies.

Objects: A rose and two rosebuds which are about to blossom (*Note*: You can use any flower and its buds, but a rose is most fitting since it is used as the symbol for life in the fight against abortion.)

Who can tell me what this flower is? *(Pause for response.)* That's right, it's a rose. It's a beautiful, living flower. Of course, I picked it now, so it won't stay alive for long, but it still is pretty, isn't it? It would be better off still growing on the rose bush it came from, but I wanted to take it along to show you. *(Let the children take a minute to look at the rose.)* I want to play a little game of pretend with this rose.

First of all, let's pretend that God says to us, "Don't pick any flowers." He didn't say that, but let's just pretend that he did. If he said that, would it be right for me to pick this rose? *(Pause for response.)* Of course not!

If God says, "Don't pick any flowers," then we shouldn't pick any flowers, right? Not even this rose. I'm glad he didn't say that. I'm glad we're just pretending. But if he did, I wouldn't have this rose here.

Now, let's pretend that this rose is a person. We'll just say that this rose stands for a person. God tells us in the Bible that we should not kill or murder anyone. Would it be right for me to murder? *(Make motions like you're going to pull the rose apart as you ask the question. Pause for response.)* Of course not. God says that we should not murder, so we should not murder. If this rose were a person, it would be wrong for me to kill it.

In fact, if this rose were a person, I should do everything I can to keep it alive and growing well, shouldn't I? I shouldn't even pick it. But it's not a person, it's a flower. And I brought it here just to remind us of living people.

Who knows what this is? *(Show them one of the rosebuds and pause for response.)* That's right, it's a bud, a rosebud. When this bud opens, it will be a rose.

In fact, it's really a rose right now, isn't it? Let's look. *(Carefully pull away a few green bracts to expose the developing petals.)* Here are the petals, all carefully wrapped up for protection. But they're still rose petals. *(If you can, pull off a few developing petals and hold them up.)* They're not dandelion petals or daisy petals. They're rose petals all right. This is really a tiny rose, all wrapped up for protection until it's strong enough to bloom as a big rose.

Now, I want you to pretend again. Pretend once more that God told us that we shouldn't pick any flowers. We already said that we would never pick this rose. *(Indicate the rose blossom.)* If God told you not to pick flowers, would you pick this rosebud? *(Hold up the bud and pause for response.)* Remember what we said: This is really a tiny rose wrapped up for protection. Should we pick this tiny, protected rose if God tells us not to pick flowers? Of course not! If God told us not to pick flowers, we simply would not pick flowers, big or small.

I'm glad we're just pretending. I'm glad that God didn't really tell us not to pick flowers, or else I couldn't have picked this rosebud to show you.

Now I want you to pretend one more time. Remember how we pretended that this rose *(indicate the rose blossom)* was a person? Now I want you to pretend that this rosebud *(indicate the rosebud)* is also a person. It's a tiny, tiny baby. It's so tiny that it's not born yet. But it's still a baby. It's just growing, protected, until it's big enough to be born.

We know that God tells us not to murder. We already said that if this rose *(indicate the rose blossom)* were a person, it would be wrong to kill it. Now, this bud is also a person, a tiny unborn baby. God said that we should not kill people. Should we kill this little, tiny rosebud, this baby waiting to be born? *(Indicate the rosebud and pause for response.)* Of course not! God told us not to kill, so we may not kill. Not big people, not small people, not even tiny babies waiting to be born.

This is a strange thing to talk about, isn't it? I'm sure none of you is going to go out and kill a little baby. Why do I talk about such things to you?

Well, there's a big word that lots of people use and argue about. You've probably already heard the word and wondered what it was. If you haven't heard the word, you will if you listen to adults talk. I want you to know about that word.

The word is *abortion*. Have you heard that word? *(Pause for response.)* Abortion is a big word that means killing little unborn babies.

Some people think that abortion—killing unborn babies—is all right to do. They talk about abortion as if it's perfectly okay.

We believe that abortion is wrong. God told us not to kill, so we should not kill—not even little unborn babies. *(Indicate the rosebud.)*

Of course, you don't have to worry about that right now, do you? I just wanted you to know what that big word is all about, so when you hear that word, you know that it means killing little babies, and that's wrong. For now, you can just look at this rose and its bud, or any flower and its bud, and remember that God made all life. And he wants us to take care of the life he makes.

51

Thanksgiving

Scripture: He makes grass grow for the cattle, and plants for man to cultivate—bringing forth food from the earth. . . . Praise the LORD (Ps. 104:14, 35).

Concept: All our food comes from God.

Objects: A pumpkin pie and a pumpkin; a can of cranberry sauce and a few cranberries (*Note:* This can be done with any prepared food and its original source. Since this lesson is for Thanksgiving, the above foods are used.)

Who can tell me what holiday we are going to have this week [what day it is today]? That's right, Thanksgiving Day! And, because Thanksgiving Day is coming [or it's Thanksgiving Day], I brought along part of my dinner.

I'd like to give you all a piece of this (*show them the pie*), but I don't want to spoil your dinners. Anyway, most of you probably have at least one of these at home. Can anyone tell me what kind of pie this is? (*Pause for response.*) Yes, it's a pumpkin pie!

Where do you think this pumpkin pie came from? *(Pause for response.)* The store? Yes, you can buy pumpkin pies at the store. My mother [spouse, I] made it? Someone made it, that's for sure. And I'll guess that your mothers, or your grandmothers, probably made your pumpkin pies.

But you can't have a pumpkin pie without putting pumpkin in it. Where does the pumpkin come from? *(Pause for response.)* That's right, pumpkins grow.

This is where pumpkin for the pie comes from. *(Show them the pumpkin.)* It comes from a vegetable called a pumpkin that grows on farms or in our gardens.

And who makes the pumpkin grow? *(Pause for response.)* That's right, God does. He sends the rain and the sun to make the pumpkin grow big and fat. Then we can pick it and make pumpkin pie from it.

If God didn't give us pumpkins, could we have pumpkin pie? So whom should we thank for pumpkins that make pumpkin pie? *(Pause for response.)* Of course, we thank God for pumpkins, just like we thank God for all our food.

Here's something else I really like to eat at Thanksgiving. *(Show them the can of cranberry sauce.)* It's cranberry sauce in a can. Not everybody likes cranberry sauce, but I do.

This can of cranberry sauce came from the store, too. But it didn't just grow on the shelf, did it? No! Someone made the cranberry sauce and put it in the can.

Does anyone know what cranberry sauce is made from? *(Pause for response.)* That's right, it's made from cranberries, just like these. *(Show them the cranberries.)* These berries once grew on low cranberry bushes.

Someone picked them when they were ripe and sent them on to the store like this. *(Indicate the whole cranberries.)* Someone picked more cranberries when they were ripe and made them into this cranberry sauce. *(Indicate the can of cranberry sauce.)* We couldn't have made the cranberry sauce without cranberries, could we?

And who makes the cranberries grow? *(Pause for response.)* You're right, God does! God gave us cranberry plants, and enough sun, and the right kind of water to make cranberries grow. If God didn't give us cranberries, we couldn't have cranberry sauce.

[*Note:* The lesson can be expanded here to include any food you wish to include. Simply follow that food back to the source, and then mention that God gives us that source.]

Do you know that all the food you will find on your table comes from God? It does! We may buy it at a store, or someone may bake it, but the food we buy and the food we prepare all comes first from God. You can trace every food back to a living plant or animal that God put on this earth and that God made grow.

I want you to try something for me today. When you sit down to eat, look at the food on your table. Then talk to your parents about it, the way we just talked about the cranberry sauce. See if you can find out which living plant or animal it came from. Then thank God for that food.

And when you get to dessert, maybe that will be pumpkin pie. Think about where that pumpkin came from and who made it grow. And thank God that he gives us all our food.

52

Why Celebrate Christmas?

Scripture: "For God so loved the world that he gave his one and only Son, that whoever believes in him shall not perish but have eternal life" (John 3:16).

Concept: We celebrate Christmas as the birth of Jesus, who brings us eternal life.

Object: A wreath made of evergreens (*Note:* If you have a wreath hanging in the sanctuary, you could have the children gather around it.)

Who can tell me what we call this green circle? *(Hold up the wreath or point to it and pause for response.)* That's right, it's called a wreath. We see a lot of wreaths, especially this time of the year. A wreath is often used in Christmas celebrations.

Can anyone show me the end of this wreath? What's the very last part that was made? Is it here? Or here? How about here? *(Point to different parts of the wreath.)* It's hard to tell. No one can say exactly where the end of this wreath is. It seems to go on forever and ever. *(Indicate the circle of the wreath several times as you say this.)* You could almost say that this wreath has no end. It just goes on and on and on.

That's why you see wreaths at Christmastime. Let me explain that a little bit.

At Christmas we celebrate the birthday of somebody very special. Can you tell me who was born on the first Christmas? *(Pause for response.)* You're right. Jesus was born on the very first Christmas. Jesus is very special.

Is Jesus an ordinary person, just like you and me? *(Shake your head as you ask the question.)* No! Jesus is much more than an ordinary person. Jesus is God.

When Jesus was born on that first Christmas, he came to earth for a special reason. He came to bring us eternal life. That means that if we really believe that Jesus is God, we will never die. Our bodies will die, but our souls, the *us* part of us, will never die. Instead, we will some day live in heaven with Jesus. We will live with him there forever.

Can you imagine forever? Can you think of a life that never ends? Nobody really can. Everything that we know has a beginning and an end. But our life with Jesus will never, ever end.

One of the few things that we can see that looks like it doesn't have an end is this wreath. *(Indicate the wreath again.)* It looks like it goes on forever. *(Indicate the circle of the wreath a few times.)*

That's why we use wreaths to celebrate Christmas. We know that we celebrate Jesus' birthday on Christmas. And this wreath can remind us of life that will go on forever *(indicate the circle of the wreath a few more times)* with Jesus.